Y0-ABJ-155

The name of Charles L. Allen spells magic not only to one of the largest Protestant congregations in America but to millions of readers who have found inspiration in his best sellers. From his home pulpit, the First Methodist Church of Houston, his fame has spread through radio and TV appearances; through his columns in *The Houston Chronicle* and *The Atlanta Journal-Constitution*; and his featured articles in some of the country's most widely read magazines. The phenomenal sales success of close to three quarters of a million copies of the author's books now in circulation is credited to his beautifully prosed answers to everyman's everyday problems. Among the most popular of his books are ALL THINGS ARE POSSIBLE THROUGH PRAYER, GOD'S PSYCHIATRY, PRAYER CHANGES THINGS and THE TOUCH OF THE MASTER'S HAND.

Life

More

Abundant

Charles L. Allen

SPIRE BOOKS

Fleming H. Revell Company
Old Tappan, New Jersey

All Scripture quotations not otherwise identified, are from the King James Version of the Bible.

The quotation from *Abe Lincoln in Illinois* by Robert Sherwood is used by permission of the publishers, Charles Scribner's Sons, copyright 1937, 1939 Robert Emmet Sherwood; renewal copyright © 1965, 1967 Madeline H. Sherwood.

The quotation from a poem by Edgar A. Guest is used by permission of Reilly & Lee, publishers.

The quotation from *He Giveth More* is from the book *The Best Loved Poems of Annie Johnson Flint* published by Evangelical Publishers, Toronto, Canada. By permission.

LIFE MORE ABUNDANT

A SPIRE BOOK
Published by Pillar Books for Fleming H. Revell Company

Spire Books edition published September 1976

ISBN: 0-8007-8258-5

Library of Congress Catalog Card Number: 68-28432

Copyright © 1968 by Fleming H. Revell Company

All Rights Reserved

Printed in the United States of America

SPIRE BOOKS are published by Fleming H. Revell Company
Old Tappan, New Jersey 07675, U.S.A.

One who lives "Life More Abundant" is
WILBUR H. DAVIES,
a sincere Christian—a great publisher—a
valued friend. With appreciation and affection
I dedicate this book to him.

The Ministry of Books

PEOPLE SMILE when I say, "I have been preaching and I have been married ever since I can remember." That is not literally true, but it comes close. I married the only girl with whom I have ever been in love. We "decided," when we were in first year college, and we married four years later. Marriage has been a wonderful experience for me.

Preaching has also been a wonderful experience, and it is literally true that I have been preaching ever since I can remember. As a little boy—four and five years old—I remember listening to my father preach. I wanted to be a preacher as he was. I recall vividly how that little boy used to slip into the church when nobody was there, put a chair behind the pulpit, stand up in it and preach to the empty pews.

When I was nineteen years old I was assigned as a pastor and, through the years, preaching has been a great joy to me. I thank God for every opportunity He has given me. I am now pastor of a church with nine thousand members, located in the heart of a great city. For nearly twenty years my sermons have been televised to countless thousands of people. I have written regularly in metropolitan newspapers, *The Atlanta Constitution, The Houston Chronicle* and others, which is a very rewarding ministry. I have had more opportunities than I can count to preach in churches and to large conventions across the country.

But I have come to the conclusion that my greatest opportunity to preach the gospel of Christ has been through the ministry of books. Every day I receive a handful of letters from people who have found something in one of my books, which, they say, has been of help. My publishers tell me that many more than a million people have bought my books, and that is an impressively large congregation.

In this little volume, I have tried to say that the religion of Christ does not take away from life, but adds to the living of each day. Some people just exist, but He came to bring us *Life More Abundant.*

Mrs. Janet Kivett, my secretary, has been very helpful in preparing this manuscript. To her I express deep appreciation.

Charles L. Allen

First Methodist Church
Houston, Texas

Contents

1.

WHY I BELIEVE IN GOD

WHEN SOMEONE asked me to preach on, "Why I Believe in God," I thought it would be easy to do. Quickly I can think of a dozen reasons to believe in God, but as I look at those reasons I know they are not my reasons. My books on theology give the arguments for God and studying those books has strengthened my faith and confirmed my beliefs. But it would not be honest for me to copy the reasons for belief in God from my books and give them as my own.

The fact is, I believed in God before I ever studied theology. The more I think about it, the more I realize I believed before I knew the reasons. I know now that it is necessary for me to breathe and that without air I would die. But long before I knew that, I just breathed.

I was born into a home where prayer was heard regularly. I did not question that there was a God to hear those prayers. I just accepted the fact. I was taken to church, and it has always seemed normal and right for me to belong to the church. Long before I knew how the church came to be, or the reasons for its existence, I felt at home in it. I am a Christian, and day by day, as I learn more about Christ, I love Him more and I praise Him more for the salvation of my soul. But I do not know when I became a Christian. For years, I have given my life to the ministry and I am sure that is what I should do. But I do not remember when I decided for the ministry. I never thought of doing anything else. I think God created me for that purpose and put it into my mind at birth.

In an American court of law, a person is presumed innocent until he is proved guilty. So it is with my own belief in God. Instead of saying I will not believe until God's exis-

11

tence is proved, I believed and I will continue to believe, until it is proved that there is no God. Until now, I have never had any cause to doubt the existence of God; thus I have never felt the necessity of trying to prove Him.

The Bible feels no necessity for proving God; it assumes God's existence. The Bible's very first words are: "In the beginning God . . ." and it goes on to give us a progressive revelation of God. Moses teaches us the laws of God; Amos reveals His justice; Hosea shows us His love; the Psalms lead us to communion with Him; Micah tells us of His ethical standards; Christ gives us the full revelation of the Father.

Jesus said to His disciples, "Let not your heart be troubled: ye believe in God . . ." (John 14:1). He did not say, "*If* you believe," or "You *should* believe." He simply said, "Ye believe" and went on to tell of the Father's house and the way to it.

God does not depend on reasons or arguments for our belief in Him. God took care of that in our creation. Call it instinct, insight, intuition, or any other name, we were born believing. As we study and learn, as we live and experience, our belief can be strengthened and enlarged. Or our belief can be perverted and misdirected. Therein lies the danger. The Ten Commandments do not command us to believe, but they do command us to keep God as the first object of our worship.

One does not need to understand God in order to believe in Him. The fact is, we understand very few things that we do. In his book, *Nature of the Physical World*, Dr. Arthur Eddington wrote: "I am standing on the threshold about to enter a room. It is a complicated business. In the first place, I must shove against an atmosphere pressing with a force of fourteen pounds on every square inch of my body. I must make sure of landing on a plank traveling at twenty miles a second round the sun. I must do this while hanging from a round planet, head outward into space." Only a few scientists bother to understand what is involved in the process of walking into a room. The rest of us just walk in.

Most of us do not understand the composition of water, but we drink it. None of us know what electricity is, but we use it. Who can understand the process of love? Yet many

12

have given their lives in sacrifice because they loved. Though we cannot explain God, most of us say with Christopher Morley: "I had a thousand questions to ask God; but when I met Him, they all fled and didn't seem to matter."

To say, "I believe in God," means more than just an intellectual assent to the existence of God. It means to trust in Him and to commit our lives to His will. I know a man who was suffering with severe headaches. He went to the doctor and his case was diagnosed as a tumor on the brain. The man had no way of knowing whether or not the doctor was correct. He had to have faith in him.

Because he had faith in the doctor, the man permitted himself to be put to sleep in a room where none of his family or friends were. He gave his consent for the doctor to open his head and cut into his brain. One slip of the knife, one tiny fraction of an inch would have meant instant death to the patient, yet he was willing to have the operation. His belief in the doctor meant he was willing and ready to trust himself to the doctor's hands.

We trust in God because we realize our own weaknesses and inadequacies. As long as we feel sufficient unto ourselves, we do not need God; we are our own God. No person ever really finds God until there is a felt need in his life that only God can fill. Until you need Him, you won't have Him.

We sometimes say it is our duty to go to church, and it is; but very few go for that reason. I would prefer that no one come to my church just from a sense of duty. The ones who gain the most from the church are those who come from a sense of need. Their minds are open to the truth of God, and their hearts are open to the presence of God. The person who comes to church really seeking God will be impressed by the very existence of the church building.

During the singing of the hymns at church, I see many people who inspire me. They have problems and burdens, but they have something else, which enables them to sing. During the time of prayer, I am impressed with the fact that so many do really pray. Surely there must be something to it.

A young lady talked to me about a job in the church. I

13

asked her what salary she expected, and she told me that salary did not matter. She said, "I will live on whatever I get. What I want is the opportunity to serve God." She inspired me, as does the memory of those, down through the centuries, who made large sacrifices for their faith. As the minister reads from the Bible and talks about it, I realize there must be a reason why the Book outlasts all other books. These and other thoughts inspire my spirit, lift my confidence, and make me surer of God.

On the other hand, if one comes to church without a sense of need, he is likely to have a cynical spirit. He finds fault with the building, he looks at the people around him and criticizes them, he doubts the sincerity of the minister, he thinks the choir is trying to show off. That person came for nothing and he receives nothing—better for him to have stayed at home.

We never really believe in God until we feel the need of Him. As Giles Fletcher put it:

He is a path, if any be misled;
He is a robe, if any naked be;
If any chance to hunger, he is bread;
If any be a bondman, he is free;
If any be but weak, how strong is he!
To dead men, life is he; to sick men, health;
To blind men, sight; and to the needy, wealth;
A pleasure without loss, a treasure without stealth.
—*Excellency of Christ*

TELL ME HOW TO BELIEVE IN GOD

"Please tell me how I can believe in God," a friend requested. This friend went on to say, "You talk about God as if everybody knew Him. But I neither know who He is, where He is, or what He does. As far as I know, I have never had any conscious dealing with God. In your sermons you say, 'Put your life in God's hands and He will carry you through.' That is like saying to one who has never flown a plane, 'Get into that jet and fly it wherever you want to go.' I do not doubt the plane's existence or its

14

ability to carry me, but I do know I cannot fly it. As for God, I am not even sure that He exists, and certainly I do not know how to 'put myself in His hands'."

In seeking a plain and straightforward answer I turned to the ninth chapter of St. Mark and read it carefully. Jesus and three of his disciples went up on the mountain and there had a marvelous experience. Before the eyes of the disciples Jesus' raiment became shining; He was transfigured before them. Then Elijah and Moses suddenly appeared and they talked together. It was so wonderful that Peter suggested they just stay on the mountain.

But Jesus knew there was work to be done in the valley below. God never gives His power to those who will not use it in service. At the foot of the mountain was a father who had brought his epileptic son. Since childhood, the boy had been afflicted. The father had asked the disciples to heal the boy but they could not. Now he asked Jesus.

Jesus said, "If thou canst believe, all things are possible to him that believeth" (Mark 9:23). Let's stop on that word "believe." What do we mean by it? "Believe" is used in at least three different senses. A person says, "I believe in the North Pole." He may not have been there, but he accepts the authority of one who has been there. Another says, "I believe that two times two is four." That is something he can reason out for himself. Thus his belief is based on his own intellect. Another says, "I believe the sunshine is warm." He has been in the sunshine and felt it; thus his belief is based on experience. Maybe he cannot explain why the sunshine is warm, but he knows it is.

There are many who sincerely want to believe in God but find it hard. Faith never comes easy, and the only way it can come is by beginning where we can begin and going on from there. No one believes in all of God. No one can. God is so great and we are so small that we can only believe in a part of Him. A man once said to Jesus, "Lord, I believe; help thou mine unbelief" (Mark 9:24). And in every person there is both belief and unbelief. No person believes completely.

The other day I stood on the beach by the ocean. The water lay before me, as far as I could see. I could feel it, I could taste the salt in it, I could swim in it and be carried

15

by the waves. I believe in the ocean because I have seen it and I have felt it. But I do not know the whole sea. I have not been with Admiral Byrd into the Arctic and Antarctic; I have not been into the tropic ocean where the mighty Amazon pours its floods out so freely.

In the ocean are mountain ranges higher and longer than any man has ever seen. There are canyons in the ocean deeper than the dry earth knows of. There is a lot of land area on the earth, but the sea is eighteeen times as large. Any man could spend his entire life studying the sea and know only a small part of it. Although we do not know it all, we can still say with assurance, "I believe in the sea."

I can say I believe in people, yet I base that belief on a very limited acquaintance. My immediate family I know intimately. I have some very close friends, and as I go about I meet what seems to me a lot of people. I have met as many as a thousand people in one week. Yet if all the people I have ever seen face to face were put together, they would represent only a very small part of the billions of people of the world. In the people I do know, however, I have seen love and faith, loyalty and unselfishness, goodness and integrity, to the extent that I do believe in people. I do not have to know every person before I learn to believe.

So I believe in God; He is so great that I can never know Him, yet He is so near that I cannot help but know Him. The Bible tells us ". . . God is love" (I John 4:8). I have loved and I have been loved. I have seen love expressed in many ways. Seeing and feeling love, I have come to believe in it. Believing in love is believing in God—a small part of God, to be sure, but still God.

Each day we can know a little more of God. We can never know all of Him, but instead of worrying about the part of God I do not know, I say, "Lord, I believe; help me to believe more."

16

2.

TO BELIEVE IN YOURSELF

I HAVE A LETTER from a lady who takes me severely to task. She attended my church service recently, and she was shocked that I did not condemn the people for their sins. She wrote me, "Most of the people there were sinners and I suspect you are a worse sinner than any of them."

Her letter disturbed me, not because of what she said, but because what she said is probably true. As I think about it, however, it seems to me we have had more than enough sermons on the sinfulness of man. Someone has wisely said, "The worst way to improve the world is to condemn it." That applies also to a person.

As Jesus stood before a sinful person one day, He said, "Neither do I condemn thee: go, and sin no more" (John 8:11). He was saying to that person, "No matter what your past has been, I still believe in you." As you read the four Gospels, you are constantly impressed by Christ's belief in people and His willingness to trust them. Over and over again He lifted people to a new sense of self-respect and to belief in themselves.

Jesus said, "If thou canst believe, all things are possible to him that believeth" (Mark 9:23). That truth applies to any person in any situation. The father of American psychology, William James, said: "In any project the one important factor is your belief. Without belief there can be no successful outcome. That is fundamental." Ralph Waldo Emerson put it this way: "Belief is absolutely necessary; no accomplishment, no assistance, no training can compensate for lack of belief."

17

Do you believe in yourself? If your answer is negative, you have a serious handicap to overcome. I assure you, however, you can learn to believe in yourself if you will take the three essential steps. The first one is: *Formulate a mental picture of yourself succeeding.*

There is an old story of an outcast beggar who was sitting across the street from an artist's studio. The artist saw him and quickly began to paint his portrait. When it was finished he called the beggar over to look at it. At first the beggar did not recognize himself. "Who is it?" he kept asking. The artist smiled and said nothing.

The beggar kept looking at the portrait until recognition began to dawn. Hesitantly he asked, "Is it I? Can it be I?" The artist replied, "That is the man I see in you." Then the beggar made a wonderful reply. "If that's the man you see," he said, "that's the man I'll be."

Sooner or later, all of us become the person we see ourselves to be. If you develop creative faith in yourself, eventually your faith will recreate you. If your mind is obsessed by thoughts of insecurity and inadequacy, it is because you have allowed such thoughts to dominate your thinking over a period of time. The only way to overcome those thoughts is by putting into your mind a positive pattern of ideas.

The first step to belief in yourself is to plant in your mind a mental picture of yourself succeeding. To start with, your mind will resist that picture. It takes much less mental effort to picture failure and our minds, like running water, seek the easiest course.

Your mind will seek to block your picture of success by building up obstacles. But over against those obstacles, think of your assets and you will see that you have more for you than against you. As you hold tenaciously to your mental picture of success, eventually your mind will accept it and gradually all your powers will focus on that picture and begin to complete it in your actual life.

If you think you are beaten, you are;
If you think you dare not, you don't.
If you want to win but don't think you can,
It's almost a cinch you won't.

If you think you'll lose, you're lost;
For out in the world we find
Success begins with a fellow's will:
It's all in the state of mind.

If you think you're outclassed, you are;
You've got to think high to rise;
You've got to be sure of yourself before
You can ever win a prize.

Life's battles don't always go
To the stronger and faster man;
But sooner or later the man who wins
Is the man who thinks he can.

—*Thinking,* Walter D. Wintle

BE WILLING TO BE YOURSELF

The second step to belief in yourself is: *Be willing to be yourself.* One of the quickest ways to depreciate yourself is to become awestruck by other people and to try to copy them. You can be *you* better than you can be anybody else. In fact, you are the only person you can be, and when you try to be somebody else, you end up frustrated and defeated.

Michelangelo once bought an inferior looking piece of marble, which no one else would buy. Asked why he bought it, he said, "Because there's an angel in there and I must set it free." Then he went to work with hammer and chisel and carved a magnificent statue of an angel.

That story reminds us of the fact that within each of us there is a finer person waiting to be set free. You do not need to be someone else; you have it within you, if you will only let it come out. As you develop your finest self, you develop marvelous self-confidence.

To believe in yourself you must take three essential steps: first, visualize yourself as succeeding; second, be willing to be yourself; and third, *Get into a right relationship with God*. Consider that third step; it is the most important of the three.

William James had a deep understanding of human nature. He said: "Every sort of energy and endurance, of courage and capacity for handling life's evils, is set free in those who have religious faith." Note what he is saying— you have energy, endurance, courage, and capacity, but religious faith is the key that unlocks these powers within you and sets them to work.

Huxley, the English scientist, said that everywhere in England, deep within the soil, are thousands of seeds of tropical plants. They have lain there dormant for years waiting for just one thing—the proper climate. If the climate of England could be changed into a tropical climate, those seeds would immediately spring up into lush, beautiful foliage.

We remember that when certain Egyptian tombs were opened some years ago, wheat was discovered in them. For four thousand years, that wheat had remained in the dry darkness of those tombs. When it was brought out and planted, it grew and produced a crop. All it needed was to be put into proper relationship with the earth, the air, and the sun.

And when you or I come into right relationship with the Spirit of God, when the warmth of His love begins to surround us and when His power begins to flow into us, the energy, endurance, courage, and capacity that have remained dormant within us begin to rise and take hold of our lives.

A father sat on the front porch of his farm home and watched a truck, driven by his own son, turn over into a ditch. He ran to the scene of the accident and found the boy pinned down under the truck in two feet of water. Although he was a small man, the father lifted that truck and pulled his son to safety. The next day he tried to lift the truck again but he couldn't move it. A doctor explained that in the moment of great need nature sent a terrific shot of adrenaline into the man's system, and he had strength he had never known before.

Almighty God built within us certain spiritual mechanisms, and when we use them rightly we have the ability to accomplish things far beyond our normal abilities. Jesus said, ". . . the kingdom of God is within you" (Luke 17:21); and He wants to bring it out. St. Paul discovered this power and he said, "I can do all things through Christ which strengtheneth me" (Philippians 4:13). Repeat those words. Repeat them *now*. Keep on repeating them until they become fixed in your mind, so fixed that doubts and fears are driven out. Also, St. Paul said, "If God be for us, who can be against us" (Romans 8:31). Really, who or what can defeat us when God is within us? Believe in God and you will believe in yourself.

3.

BE WILLING TO BE YOURSELF

THE FIRST STEP toward happiness and success in life is this: Be willing to be yourself. As Robert Louis Stevenson put it, "To be what we are, and to become what we are capable of becoming, is the only end of life." I think the major cause of frustration, failure, and unhappiness is our unwillingness to accept ourselves and be ourselves.

In the first place, not to be willing to be yourself is an insult to God. Consider these two statements from the Bible: "All things were made by him; and without him was not any thing made that was made" (John 1:3). "All things" includes me and you. Jesus said, ". . . as my Father hath sent me, even so send I you" (John 20:21).

21

Before you were born, you existed in the mind of God. He decided that the world needed you at a certain time—that there is something for you to do that is different from what any other person will do. Everything God made has its own peculiar identity. There are billions of blades of grass, but no two alike. No two snowflakes have ever been identical.

No person who ever existed is exactly like you. Even the print of your little finger is separate and distinct. It should lift you to a new realization of importance to know that of all the billions of people the earth has known, there is only one of you.

A sixth-grade teacher asked her class, "What is here in the world today that was not here fifteen years ago?" She expected them to name new inventions. One little boy held up his hand. "What is it, Johnny, that was not here fifteen years ago?" He replied, "Me." He was right. Something new came into the world when you were born. Something that God planned and wanted.

My Best Possible Self

Second, when I accept myself as myself, I begin working to become my best possible self. God made some men with mechanical abilities and some with artistic abilities; He made some women beautiful and some homely; He made some people short and others tall. While we can improve and develop, none of us can really change ourselves. Long ago, I accepted the idea that God made me to be a preacher. Also, I accepted the idea that I wasn't made to be a Peter Marshall, a Norman Vincent Peale, or a Ralph Sockman. He made those men to do their work. As much as I may wish it were different, I also accepted the idea that I was made to be Charles Allen. So, the only thing left for me to do is do the best with Charles Allen that I can. That is also true for you.

Willingness to be yourself will rid your life of all jealousy and envy. It will eliminate all feelings of inferiority. It will set you free for the giving of yourself to life as you have opportunity, without fear of failure or defeat. When you really decide to be yourself, you know you can succeed. That is the one thing you can do. When you secretly want to be someone else—that is when you become unhappy and begin to fail.

Every person is really two selves—the self he is and the self he has the possibility of becoming. Highest success will come to you when you begin to picture in your mind your best possible self.

Someone asked Thomas Edison how he accounted for his amazing inventive genius. He replied, "It is because I never think in words, I think in pictures." He pictured in his mind some object he desired to invent. This picture then took possession of him. It sank into his subconscious mind and, even while he was thinking of something else, his subconscious mind worked on it. Because the subconscious mind has marvelous creative power, he got flashes of insight—"creative hunches" he called them—and that accounted for his greatness.

A successful short-story writer told me that he always wrote his stories backwards. First he wrote the ending, and then he wrote the story to fit it. That is a good way to look at your own life. Get in mind the ending, your highest goal, and then you will naturally make your life the story to fit it.

Harold Sherman tells about a miserable, miserly lady who saved her money, but finally lost everything. She told him, "What I have feared has come. Here I am old and penniless. Now there is nothing for me but the poorhouse." He rebuked her: "There you go again. You thought poverty, you feared poverty, you pictured poverty until it came. Now you want the poorhouse. Keep thinking about it and that is exactly what you will get."

Being a wise counselor, he led her to think positively. She didn't regain her lost wealth, but she did later become employed as a companion to a woman of wealth, and as such she traveled widely and was happier than she had ever been before. Yes, you must be yourself, but be sure to think in terms of your best possible self.

Let me give you a simple plan that works:

(1) Write down exactly what you want. Be specific and clear; don't deal in vague generalities. Keep working on it

until you can state your goals in life in a hundred words or less. Be sure that is what you want.

(2) Read in your Bible Mark 11:24. "What things soever ye desire, when ye pray, believe that ye receive them, and ye shall have them." This is not as "magical" as it first sounds. If your desires are unreasonable and not according to the will of God, it will not be possible for you to believe.

(3) Read what you have written aloud to yourself at least twice each day, until it becomes the dominating thought in your mind. Let the picture take complete possession of you, and then you will give yourself completely to that picture.

This may sound simple, but I tell you the results can be amazing.

THE BLESSED COMPANIONSHIP

When I was a pastor in Atlanta, the church contracted with a firm in England for twenty-five stained-glass windows, presenting the life of Christ. It was not too difficult to decide on the particular scenes to be used, except in one case.

Which scene from His life should be in the window back of the pulpit? Since that was the window the people would be looking into as they worshiped, we wanted to be sure it was the right one. What would it be? His birth? The Lord preaching, praying? The shepherd? The Last Supper? The cross? His resurrection? Any of those would have been appropriate, but we did not select any of them.

Just before His ascension, He said to His disciples, "Go ye . . . and, lo, I am with you alway . . ." (Matthew 28:19-20). This is the one we decided on for the focal point in the church. Think about it. These disciples had committed so many blunders and they were limited men in so many ways. They had even denied their Lord and had acted in a cowardly and shameful fashion. But in spite of that, Jesus was willing to trust His work into their hands and He promised His Presence and Power to them. Those men never faltered after that. When we believe ourselves to be

24

within the will of God and know He is helping us, we will not fail.

"Lo, I am with you alway." That assurance gives to one a sense of conquering support. Recently, I was talking with a man who gives all of his time to financial campaigns. His company has been doing that work for many years, and they know a lot about it. One rule they insist on is that solicitors go out in pairs. After much experience, they have learned that two solicitors working together will raise four times as much money as one going alone.

Jesus understood that principle, and when He sent His disciples out, you remember, the Bible tells us, "And he called unto him the twelve, and began to send them forth by two and two" (Mark 6:7). There is strength in companionship. Just before Christ ascended, He gave them the assurance that He would be with them. They believed and did not doubt, and because of His Presence, they became conquerors of the world.

The realization of His Presence gives us guidance. A man gave me this testimony: He was in serious difficulty. He thought about what he should do, but everything he tried seemed to fail. One day he asked himself, "What would Christ do?" He asked that question honestly. That is, in asking he was also committing himself to the answer, whatever it might be. He found the answer, and now that question has become the habit of his life.

"What would Christ do?" When we accept for ourselves the answer to that question, our shoulders straighten up, our eyes light up, power overcomes our weakness, and victory drives away our defeat. We look life straight in the eye as we say, "I can do all things through Christ which strengtheneth me" (Philippians 4:13).

4.

HOW TO OVERCOME
AN INFERIORITY COMPLEX

"How to overcome an Inferiority Complex." That is something nearly every person would like to know. Most of us have moments when we feel defeated and inadequate. We often feel inferior as we face the circumstances of our lives.

In the hospital the other day, a man I was visiting said to me, "It's no use. This thing is bigger than I am and I can't handle it." His doctor says he could make a complete recovery if he could only begin to believe in himself. But he has accepted the idea of defeat and has surrendered to it. It is much easier to surrender to an inferiority complex than to overcome it, and a lot of people have done just that.

But to those who really want to gain confidence and power, who are unwilling to give up and quit, I can show the path to follow. You will find it in the seventeenth chapter of I Samuel. There were two armies at war. One was encamped on a mountain on one side of a valley; the other was on a mountain on the opposite side. At that time there was a lull in the fighting.

One morning there came out of the Philistines' camp a man by the name of Goliath. He was a tremendous man, whose height was six cubits and a span. He wore a helmet of brass, a coat of iron, and heavy coverings on his legs. In one hand he carried a long spear, and in the other hand an enormous shield. He was a fearful-looking fellow. In fact, he was a giant.

He cried out to the armies of Israel, challenging them to select a man to come forward and do battle. The story says, 'When Saul and all Israel heard those words of the Philistine, they were dismayed, and greatly afraid" (17:11). Goliath gave that entire army an inferiority complex. Notice again those words, ". . . they were dismayed, and greatly afraid." You couldn't describe the effects of an inferiority complex better if you wrote a book about it.

In the army of Israel were several sons of Jesse. The father was concerned about his sons so one day he sent David, the youngest, to carry some extra food to his brothers. Also, he was to see how the boys were getting along. To visit the camp of the army must have been a thrilling mission for young David. He found his brothers and, as they were talking, big Goliath came out and issued his challenge to fight. David saw how the men "fled from him, and were sore afraid" (17:24).

So David went to Saul and volunteered to fight Goliath. Saul laughed and said, ". . . thou art but a youth. . . ." Then David told the King how he had slain both a lion and a bear that had come to attack his sheep. He told the King how God had given him strength in those fights. And now he had reason to believe that God would help him in his fight against Goliath.

The King was persuaded by the courageous confidence of young David and gave his permission. Down the mountain and across the valley toward Goliath David marched.

WE ALL FACE GIANTS

David is not the last person to be confronted by a giant. In fact, we all have our giants and that is why so many people develop inferiority complexes. If there were no giants, you would not feel inferior.

We remember how the children of Israel came to the border of their Promised Land. They appointed a committee to spy out the land. They found it to be a good land, "flowing with milk and honey," and they so much wanted to possess it. The majority reported, however, "there we saw giants, and we were in our own sight as grasshoppers" (Numbers 13:33).

Some of the giants in our lives are real. Others are imaginary. But whether they are real or not, the trouble comes

27

when we allow the giants to make us as grasshoppers, "dismayed and afraid"; when, instead of giving our best, we give up and quit. Your giant may be some physical handicap; it may be a hard job that is before you; it may be a deep sorrow, a financial debt, a feeling of loneliness, a harmful habit, or one of many things. David did not minimize the strength of the giant, but neither did he let the giant minimize him. The first step in overcoming an inferiority complex is to consider your own strength and power, as well as the strength of the adversary in your life.

FACE UP TO YOUR GIANT

The second step is to go forth and do battle with the giant. You will never win a fight if you don't fight. Before David went forth to battle, he decided how best he could do it. Saul took off his own armor and put it on David. I can see in my mind this boy wearing Saul's brass helmet and coat of iron. Then he took Saul's sword in his hand. But Saul's armor didn't fit David. More than that, this shepherd boy did not know how to use that big sword. So he took off the armor and handed it back.

That was the wisest thing David could have done. He realized that he had to fight the giant in his own way. So he took a sling out of his pocket, gathered up five stones and went forth. There is a great lesson to learn. One reason many people have an inferiority complex is that they try to be somebody else instead of just themselves. If God had wanted you to be like someone else, He would have made you like that. Instead, He made you as you are and He expects you to be yourself.

When I started out to preach, I felt that I wanted to be like my father. I still would like to be as he was. I have every sermon he ever wrote, but I have never used one of them. I would if I could because they are better than my sermons, but I don't have his personality; and if I tried to use his sermons, I would fail completely. Instead, I must use my own personality and write my own sermons and have confidence in my own way of doing things.

Suppose David had said, "All I have is a sling, so I can't

28

fight." He would have failed miserably. The secret of success is to determine what you have and then have the courage and energy to use it.

When David went out to meet Goliath, it seemed to be a hopeless fight for him, a young shepherd boy facing a mighty giant trained in the art of warfare. In addition, the giant was fully armed while David had only a sling and some small stones. The Bible says Goliath "disdained him," cursed him and vowed to feed his flesh to the fowls of the air and the beasts of the field.

David was not afraid, however. Very calmly he replied to the giant, and his reply is one of the most sublime expressions of faith in the entire Bible. He said, "Thou comest to me with a sword, and with a spear, and with a shield: but I come to thee in the name of the Lord of hosts . . ." (I Samuel 17:45).

Carefully David placed the stone in his sling. He began to whirl it around his head; he took aim and let it go. That stone found its mark on the giant's forehead. He fell on his face. David had five stones, but he needed only one. If we use what we have, it is generally true that we have more than we actually need to win the victory.

Then David went over and put his foot on the fallen giant, took the giant's own sword, and cut off his head at the shoulders. That was pretty drastic but it was the custom in those days. When the Philistines saw what had happened, they took to their heels. The army of Israel gained courage from David, and they took out after them and routed them. And Saul, when he saw what had happened, made David his assistant. Later David became the king.

It is a great story. It has meaning for the twentieth century. We may read a hundred books on psychology, but we won't find a better way of overcoming an inferiority complex.

The Saturday afternoon before I was to preach my first sermon as pastor of Grace Church in Atlanta, I was in the church alone. It seemed so big and strange to me that I was almost paralyzed by fear. I was much younger then and I knew nothing about a big city church. I knew I would fail miserably. Then I walked down the aisle and knelt at the altar and prayed. I felt a calm spirit coming over me, and I left the church that day with joy and peace in my heart.

At the close of my sermon the next night, I told of my experience and gave opportunity to those present to come and pray at the altar. I repeated that invitation every Sunday night for the twelve years I was pastor of that church. Thousands did as I did and went out of the church to face the tasks of the coming week with confidence and without fear.

When one stands at his full height in the face of obstacles, when one refuses to shrink back but instead gives his own best, when one sincerely says to life, "I come to you in the name of the Lord," the inhibitions are taken away, the tangles are cleared, and the clouds of life are lifted.

5.

VICTIMS OF
THE OBSTACLE COMPLEX

VAST NUMBERS of people are victims of the obstacle complex. These people have become convinced that certain difficulties or circumstances stand in their way and that it is impossible for them to reach the goals in life they most want. Let me illustrate with one of the classic examples of history.

The children of Israel were in bondage in Egypt, but God had put into their minds the vision of a better life. He had promised them a land—a land in which they would have all that they wanted. During their hard labor and extreme want, they were sustained by the hope of their Promised Land. Finally the day came when their dreams began to come true.

At least they made a start. Under the leadership of Moses, they threw off the bondage of Pharaoh and moved out of Egypt. It was a long and painful journey of forty years, but along the way they had many evidences of the power of God. He divided the Red Sea and brought them safely out on the other side; He guided them through the wilderness with a pillar of cloud by day and of fire by night. He provided food day by day.

Finally, they reached the very border of their Promised Land. There they stopped to ask questions. That was their first mistake. They began to ask, "Can we possess the land?" God had promised it to them; again and again, He had proved His power and His willingness to help them, but now they hesitated. For nine generations, they had been in bondage; for forty years, they had struggled across the wilderness—why did they hesitate on the border? They had everything to gain and nothing to lose, but still they hesitated.

Shakespeare was right when he said:

> There is a tide in the affairs of men
> Which, taken at the flood, leads on to fortune;
> Omitted, all the voyage of their life
> Is bound in shallows and in miseries.
> —*Julius Caesar*, Act IV, Scene 3

They appointed a committee of twelve to spy out the land. The committee reported it was a good land, "flowing with milk and honey." Caleb spoke up and said, "Let us go up at once, and possess it; for we are well able to overcome it." But others on the committee said, "We be not able to go up against the people; for they are stronger than we. . . . And there we saw the giants . . . and we were in our own sight as grasshoppers . . ." (Numbers 13:30-33).

It is a lot easier to surrender to giants than it is to fight them, so they stopped. They became victims of the obstacle complex. They murdered their opportunity; they lost their chance.

That isn't an old story. It is as new as today's newspaper.

31

We dream of being something better. We believe God wants us to have the more abundant life. We have every assurance of His help. But we see obstacles in the way and we become shrinking cowards, saying, "I can't," "It's impossible," "It isn't for me"; and we hesitate; we stop; we lose out.

Remember: success comes in *cans,* failure in *can'ts.* So, get hold of a *can*-opener and start using it.

Whoever you are, there are three basic facts that you can depend on. First, God has for you a "promised land." Second, there will be difficulties in your way. Third, with your own ability and God's help, you can be the person God intends and reach the goals in life that God has shown you through your hopes and dreams.

In truth, each one of us is standing, right at this moment, at the exact spot on which the children of Israel once stood, on the very border of our promised land. But it is also true that vast numbers never really possess their land. They end up frustrated, defeated, and miserable. Why do people fail to reach the top of their abilities in life? There are three reasons:

WE CONCONTRATE ON OBSTACLES
INSTEAD OF STRENGTHS

First, they concentrate on the obstacles in their way instead of on their strengths. "We saw giants standing between us and our Promised Land," the children of Israel said. And we say the same thing. The fact is that every person has had obstacles to overcome.

Whenever I get discouraged, I like to think about some of the great names in history and the giants they faced. Sir Walter Scott limped through life on club feet. Napoleon was an epileptic. John Milton, who wrote *Paradise Lost,* was blind, as was Homer, the great Greek poet.

Louisa May Alcott, who wrote *Little Women,* a book that has been read by millions, was told by an editor that she had no writing ability and advised to stick to her sewing. When Walt Disney submitted his first drawings for publication, the editor told him he had no talent. The teachers of Thomas A. Edison said he was too stupid to learn. F. W. Woolworth built a great chain of stores, but when he was twenty-one years old he was not permitted to wait on the customers in the store where he worked. His employers said he did not have sense enough to meet the public. Josiah Wedgwood, whose name stands for lovely china, was a lame, uneducated, neglected boy. Beethoven was deaf. Before Admiral Richard E. Byrd flew over the North Pole and the South Pole, he was retired from the United States Navy as unfit for service.

But we say, "Others could overcome their obstacles, but my case is different." The only difference is that some people fight to overcome their obstacles, while others sit back and let their obstacles overcome them. Some people live on top of the world; others live with the world on top of them.

"We saw giants—we are as grasshoppers," said the children of Israel. Remember this fact: If you concentrate on your obstacles, they will grow into giants and you will sink into a grasshopper. But if you concentrate on your powers, you will become the giant and your obstacles will become like grasshoppers. It depends on which view you decide to take.

WE ARE NOT WILLING TO PAY THE PRICE

A second reason why we fail to possess our individual life's promised land is that we are not willing to pay the price.

There is a wonderful life within reach of every person— our promised land. God put it into our dreams; He gave us the ability to hope. But promised lands never come cheaply.

A boy told me the other day he had to give up his hopes of a college education because he didn't have enough money. I thought back to the days when I was in college. I remember a boy who made his way through college by milking twenty cows every morning before breakfast and every afternoon before supper. Another one got up every morning at three o'clock and worked four hours as a night watchman. I thought of many I know today who work all day and then go to school at night.

Too many young people today, when they look for a job, are only concerned about two things—the number of hours and the amount of the salary. But a few people forget hours and think of opportunity.

God has a promised land for you, but it remains for you to say with Caleb of old, "Let us go up at once, and possess it; for we are well able to overcome it" (Numbers 13:30). Caleb believed in himself, and he was willing to fight the battles, but he had still a third thing: He had faith in God.

Use Your Faith

If there is some obstacle blocking the pathway to your promised land, whether it be lack of opportunity, some opposition, or some personal weakness, read again Jesus' words in Matthew 17:20: "If ye have faith as a grain of mustard seed, ye shall say unto this mountain, Remove hence to yonder place; and it shall remove; and nothing shall be impossible unto you."

There is hardly anything smaller than a mustard seed, and there is hardly anything larger than a mountain. And through the use of those two illustrations, Jesus is saying a little faith can have large consequences. When you face a mountain of fear, or of handicaps, or of difficulties in your home life, or of an unhappy job, or of monthly bills—remember the Lord said, faith moves mountains.

And how does one go about getting faith? I quoted Jesus' statement about faith and mountains. He said it to a group of people who had failed at a task. Then in the very next verse He said, ". . . this kind goeth not out but by prayer. . . ." Prayer is the food of faith. Why is that so? Because prayer is the doorway into the Presence of God.

Before a great battle, Napoleon would stand alone in his tent and one by one his marshals would enter, grasp his hand in silence and go out again. In his book, *Learning to Have Faith*, Dr. John A. Redhead has this wonderful line: "Power comes from the Presence, and the way to power is the practice of the Presence."

Tonight when you say your prayers, take your mind off your obstacles and think of God. Say, "I can do all things through Christ which strengtheneth me" (Philippians 4:13). Keep saying it over and over until you get the feel of it. Say, "If God be for us, who can be against us" (Romans 8:31). Say it so many times that it begins to take possession of you. And as you possess faith and become possessed by faith, you will at the same time begin to possess your promised land.

6.

WAITING FOR
OUR PROMISED LAND

FOR GENERATIONS the children of Israel were slaves in Egypt. They were forced to do the most menial work and live under the most humiliating circumstances. It was hard for them to bear that bondage.

They were a proud people, descendants of the greatest men of history. In their veins flowed noble blood. In them was the stuff of poets and prophets. Making brick as slaves was unnatural for those people. How they must have resented being in Egypt! But they were sustained by a promise of God, His promise of a land of their own where they could follow the way of life they were created for. They lived on hope—hope based on their belief in the faithfulness of God.

But for nine generations they were kept in slavery. Surely they grew weary in waiting. Why were they held back so long? Perhaps God was waiting for a Moses to rise up. Maybe God had to wait until the people were ready to follow His leadership. Even after they left Egypt, they were forced to wander forty long years in the wilderness. But during those forty years they were in training, developing their laws and their power to govern themselves.

Even at the border of the Promised Land, they had to

wait—to wait until they were willing to pay the price to possess their land. It was Mohammed who said, "Whatever God hath ordained, can only be attained by striving." They saw giants in their Promised Land, and they shrank from fighting them. Promised lands never come cheaply. There are always difficulties in the way of possessing them. But finally the children of Israel did come into their own Promised Land.

JESUS HAD TO WAIT

That story is about a group of people, but it is just as true for the individual person. Look at the most thrilling example of all time, the story of Christ. He said, ". . . I must be about my Father's business . . ." (Luke 2:49); "I came . . . not to do mine own will, but the will of him that sent me" (John 6:38); ". . . he that hath sent me is with me" (John 8:29).

As some poet has said:

> Jesus, too, had a Promised Land,
> But it wasn't a place,
> It was a plan.

A plan for His life, a work to be done, a place to be filled; God's plan for Christ was the establishment of a kingdom—the Kingdom of God. It meant the creating on earth of a society in which love, peace, and righteousness would reign. It was a thrilling and glorious way to spend one's life.

Yet Jesus, too, had to wait in some land of bondage. His Egypt was a carpenter's shop. Circumstance was the pharaoh that held Him in captivity. No doubt Joseph had died when Jesus was a teen-age boy. On His shoulders fell the responsibility of earning a living for Himself and Mary and his smaller brothers and sisters. No doubt His ambition was to go to college, but He forever lost that chance. Circumstances stood in the way of His dreams and brought disappointment instead of fulfillment.

Jesus had to wait, and wait, and wait to get out of bondage and to journey toward His promised land. But maybe the waiting was part of God's plan for His Son.

Within the breast of Christ was burning a fire. It was the consciousness of God's plan for His life. Surely He was anxious to get started, to see results, to achieve His life's purpose. But circumstances held Him in slavery.

Instead of preaching the good news of the Kingdom, He was forced to saw planks and hammer nails. It was such menial work for the Son of God to be doing. It caused Him to miss going to college. Every day He was held back, it seemed, was a day lost. But the days went into months and into years, and still He had to wait. His chance did not come until He was thirty years old. In those days, thirty years old was approaching old age.

But as you study His entire life, you begin to feel that the waiting was part of God's plan. Certainly Jesus used His circumstances in the finest possible way. Instead of becoming bitter, instead of surrendering His dreams, instead of turning to some lesser purpose, He held fast to His promised land and at the same time was faithful to life, day by day. As we study His later ministry, we see that the opportunities of His limited "today" became the stones out of which He built His castle tomorrow.

He became trained and conditioned in the school of experience, instead of in college. I don't know what the scholars might have taught Him, but we do know many of the things He learned day by day, and we know how He used His knowledge for the glory of God.

Someone imagines that one day a farmer came to him for estimates on the building of a new barn. While at Jesus' shop, the farmer boasted loudly of his great abundance and talked profanely about the kind of life he lived. But the next week that farmer's son came to Jesus to get a coffin made in which to bury his father. As Jesus made the coffin, He thought about that man and the mistakes he had made. Later Jesus was not in the carpenter's shop; instead He was preaching to the multitudes. He saw in them a mad desire for things. He remembered that farmer of past years and He told them the story (Luke 12:16-21). It was a story they could understand, and by the use of that experience, Jesus taught the truth of God.

So it was with all of those matchless stories He told. They came out of life, His own life, and they had great meaning for the people. In the school of experience Jesus learned well the lessons of life, and as a result, the Bible says, ". . . the common people heard him gladly" (Mark 12:37). Being able to win the common people, helped Him gain the followers who would carry on His work.

In many instances the handicaps, frustrations, and disappointments of life hold us in bondage and away from the realization of our highest purposes. Yet it is also true that as we are faithful day by day, the life circumstances we are forced to live with prepare us for the possession of our own personal promised land.

WE HAVE TO WAIT, TOO

We believe God has a plan for each of our lives. But just as the children of Israel were held back from the Promised Land by their bondage in Egypt, and just as Jesus was delayed so long in His mission by the cirumstances that forced Him to work in a carpenter's shop, so do we sometimes feel enslaved by the circumstances and frustrations of life.

One day Moses came to lead the children of Israel out of bondage, and one day Jesus closed the door of His shop for the last time and went forth preaching. But the question for many people is, 'Will the moment of release ever come for me?"

First, let me say, as Browning said, in *Pippa Passes*, "All service ranks the same with God." It is not the work we do, but the spirit within us that determines our real lives. If work is done in the spirit of consecration, it is just as sacred to sell soap as it is to preach sermons, or to be a butcher as it is to be a bishop. Your present work can be done for the glory of God—but there is something more to be said.

Second, for every person who is faithful to the living of each day, there will come an hour of destiny—a time of self-fulfillment. It will come, I emphasize, if we remain faithful to the daily tasks without losing heart or hope. No member of God's team trains for the race without one day being given a chance to run. Sooner or later God says to every person who is ready, "Now—now your moment has come."

We remember that Jesus said to His disciples, ". . . as my Father hath sent me, even so send I you" (John 20:21). But to them He also said, ". . . tarry ye in the city of Jerusalem, until ye be endued with power from on high" (Luke 24:49). That is, God will use you when you become consecrated to His will and purposes and possess His Spirit.

Here is an illustration. A great violinist thrilled his audience with his playing. At the end of the selection, he smashed the violin into a hundred pieces over a chair. The people sat aghast. Then he picked up another violin and said, "Don't be alarmed. The one I smashed was purchased for only a few dollars in a shop down the street. I shall now play upon my Stradivarius." He played the same selection but the majority of the people could not tell the difference.

Then the violinist said, "Friends, so much has been said about the value of my violin that I wanted to impress upon you the fact that the music is not in the instrument; it is in the one who plays upon it."

So it is with us. Our talents are varied. Many of us are conscious of our limitations. We are tempted to feel we are too unimportant to matter. But when we put ourselves into God's hands, when His purposes become our purposes, when we pray, ". . . nevertheless not my will, but thine, be done" (Luke 22:42), the great Master of us all will be able to produce through the lives of each of us the great music of life. But He cannot use a life until it is put into His hands.

7.

THERE IS A DIFFERENCE BETWEEN YOU AND YOUR ACTIONS

"THOU SHALT LOVE thy neighbour as thyself," said Jesus (Matthew 19:19). Let's take that sentence apart and look at it more closely. "Thou shalt love"—that seems like a contradiction in terms. "Thou shalt" is a command, and a command implies force. An officer in the army issues a command to a soldier. Maybe the soldier does not wish to comply with the command, but he does it anyway. The soldier uses his will power to force himself to obey.

But can love be commanded? Even if it could, who would want to receive someone's commanded love? Sometimes we command our children to turn off the television and study their lessons. They don't want to do it but after some argument, if they decide we really mean what we say, they will obey reluctantly. A child can be made to study, whether he wants to or not. Suppose I say to my children, "I command you to love me." No, we think love must come as a result of something else other than the force of command. Yet Jesus said, "Thou shalt love."

Who does Jesus command us to love? "Thy neighbor," He says. Once a man asked the question, "Who is my neighbor?" In reply Jesus told him a story about a Samaritan, a man of another race. If you are a white person and asked Him that question, He might tell you a story about a Negro. If you are a Protestant, He might tell you about a Catholic. If you hold resentment in your heart toward some person, our Lord might make that very person the center of a story telling you who your neighbor is. Ask Jesus, "Who is my neighbor?" He will point to the one you resent the most and say, "There is your neighbor." "Thou shalt love thy neighbor," Jesus said.

"As thyself," our Lord said we should love. Here we have the key that unlocks the door to the meaning of this command to love. Every person loves himself or herself. Self-love is both normal and right. Jesus does not condemn our love. In fact, the clear implication of His command commends and upholds self-love. Yet self-love does not always mean self-approval. In one of his poems, Edgar A. Guest says:

> I don't want to stand with the setting sun
> And hate myself for the things I've done.

DISTINCTION BETWEEN SELF AND ACTIONS

We don't ever really hate ourselves, but very often we do hate the things we have done. Sometimes our actions are stupid; sometimes they are selfish; sometimes they are bad tempered. In looking back at such actions, we feel shame, regret, and even hate. We despise the thing we have done or said, yet at the same time we continue to love ourselves. You see, we make a distinction between ourselves and our actions.

Certainly we allow that distinction in reference to our own selves. We do something that is not right and that is beneath our standards, and we say, "That was not the real me." "I am ashamed of what I did," we say.

Will Rogers used to say, "I have never met a man I did not like." That statement needs interpretation. Most of us meet a person we don't like every time we look in the mirror. That is, we have weaknesses that we don't like and wish we were rid of. We remember things we have said and done that we don't like and wish we could change.

Even in the best friend you have, you see some things you don't like. Some people's faults are so offensive to you that you feel you thoroughly dislike that person. When you look more closely, however, you realize it is the person's actions rather than the person that you dislike. We recall

41

how Jesus said of the Prodigal Son, "And when he came to himself . . ." (Luke 15:17).

That boy was thoroughly selfish and he lived in a selfish spirit. Nobody likes that. But when we realize it was not the real person who was acting that way, we forgive his actions and we love him in spite of what he did. When Jesus commands, "Love thy neighbour as thyself," He doesn't mean that we must like everything someone else does. He does mean we must not hold hatred or ill will in our hearts against the real person. It means more—because love is an active force rather than just an emotional feeling. To love means to give ourselves in every possible opportunity of service. The emotion of love cannot be commanded, but service of love can be. And if the service of love is sincere, eventually we will feel the emotion of love.

Let me use the finest illustration the world has ever seen. It is Christ on the cross. Certainly He did not like the actions of certain people that day. They were cruel and crude; they were heartless and very unfair. Christ could never like such actions. Yet He looked beyond their actions and He saw them. While He hated the sin, He loved the sinner. Since love always expresses itself in the best way that it can under the circumstances, Christ did something even for those who were crucifying Him. He prayed for the forgiveness of their sins. He always expressed His love.

When a leper came, though He did not like leprosy, He healed and blessed the man. To a paralytic He said, "Thy sins be forgiven." When He saw Zacchaeus, certainly He did not like the thieving trickery of the man, yet He took time to help him find the better way. Christ said ". . . he that hath seen me hath seen the Father . . ." (John 14:9). Sometimes I look at certain people and I wonder how even God could love them. Then I think of myself, and with even greater wonder do I realize He loves me. Remembering His love for me helps me to obey His command to love my fellowman, no matter what he may have done.

A LADY WHO FORGAVE

When I was preaching in a series of services in Florida, a

lady phoned asking to see me. She seemed in distress, but I could not possibly free any time for her until after the service that night. I promised to talk with her then. When I did meet her, she was smiling and so happy she seemed to bubble over.

I asked, "Are you sure you're the lady who phoned me this morning?" She said, "Yes, but I don't need your help now, so I won't keep you." I said, "When a person has changed as completely as you have, I want to know what happened." So we sat down on the front pew of the church and she told me her story.

Her husband died suddenly leaving no money or insurance for the support of their four children and herself. He did have, however, a small electrical supply business. In the business was a man her husband had trained for six years. She felt she could carry on the business with that man's help.

She had one competitor in the community and that man tried to buy her out, offering only a fraction of what her business was worth. When she wouldn't sell, he became angry and told her he would force her out. He cut prices and did everything he could against her, yet she held on. Then one day, the man her husband had trained told her he was quitting. He was going to work for the other man, who had offered him more salary than she could pay.

She carried on by herself as best she could, but it was a struggle. Sometimes her children did not have enough to eat. Worse was the hatred she had in her heart against that man. Hate is poison both for our souls and our bodies, and she knew that. Yet she could not seem to do anything about it. It was in such a situation she had phoned me that morning. That night, she arranged for a neighbor to sit with her children and she came to church to talk with me about it after the service.

My sermon that night was on the cross. I told about how through the power of mental television—imagination and memory—we can actually see back across the years. In detail, I described how He prayed in Gethsemane, the coming of the soldiers, the betraying kiss of one He had trusted, His trials before Herod and Pilate. I told about His humiliation before that mob as they stripped off His clothes, how

43

they drove the nails, hung Him up to die, and then spit on Him, mocked and ridiculed.

I took about forty-five minutes to describe that picture as vividly as I could. Then I said, "Listen! He is about to speak!" We strained our ears, and across the centuries His voice came clear and strong, saying, "Father, forgive them." Then I invited those present to come to the altar and pray.

This woman told me that as she knelt, the only thing she could think of was the man she hated. She found herself praying for him. She prayed the prayer the Master prayed. She felt cleansed and whole again. She told me that now she had no fear of the future. When Christ comes into our hearts, we can love even as He loved.

8.

THE KEY TO UNLOCK YOURSELF

THERE IS A POOR fellow in the Bible who has my sympathy. He was given a talent, which represented ability and opportunity. True, he was not given as many talents as some others, but he did have at least one. He could have amounted to something. Instead he explained to his Lord, ". . . I was afraid, and went and hid thy talent in the earth . . ." (Matthew 25:25).

A lot of people today are like that man. They have buried themselves in some prison of hopelessness, despair, and uselessness. "I was afraid," the man said. A physician kept a record over a period of years of the fears of his patients. He found that 40 percent were afraid of things that never happened; 30 percent were afraid because of past events about which they could do nothing; 12 percent were afraid of some imaginary illness; 10 percent were afraid of something that might happen to some loved one. Only 8 percent of the fears had real causes—92 percent of the fears were needless. Yet real or unreal, fear can cause you to become a locked-up person, unhappy and useless.

What is the key that will unlock yourself? Long years ago, the prophet Isaiah was concerned about the future of his people. He assured them that if they would seek God's guidance, they would find it. He said, "And thine ears shall hear a word behind thee, saying, This is the way, walk ye in it . . ." (Isaiah 30:21). Until one hears and obeys that voice, he is never set entirely free.

It is a matter of making up your mind once and for all that you will accept God's will for your life no matter what it is. But before you can hear God's voice, you must make the commitment. God doesn't bargain with us. He expects us to trust Him to the point of absolute surrender. The Prodigal Son didn't say to the father, "Before I decide to come back home, I want to know what you will expect of me." Instead, he came saying, ". . . make me as one of thy hired servants" (Luke 15:19). Make me—make me—make me. He surrendered to the father's will.

You Begin to Walk

When you decide God's way shall be your way, immediately you begin to walk. You stop worrying about whether you will fail or not; you just launch out on faith. There is a story of a young bear cub who was puzzled about how to walk. The little bear said to its mother, "Shall I move my right foot first, or my left, or my two front feet together, or the ones on the left side together and then the ones on the right side?" The mother bear said, "Leave off thinking about it and just walk."

We think about this problem and that one, about the future and where it might lead, and we get so confused we don't know which way to move. But when we say with Christ, "Thy will be done," we do see at least the first step and we find the strength to take that step. At this very moment say with me, "Now I yield my life to God's will, whatever His will may be." That is surrender, but surren-

45

der based on high faith and surrender that leads to complete victory.

You Turn From the Unhappy Past

Complete yielding to the will of God is the key that will open the tomb of your buried self and set you to really living. That commitment will take all the fears out of your life, because it turns your face away from your unhappy past and causes you to face the future with anticipation instead of apprehension.

The realization of being within God's will immediately rids your mind of any thought of failure. I refer frequently to the experiment the Coués used many years ago. They would place a plank twelve inches wide on the ground and invite people to walk it. Anyone could walk that. Then they would place that same plank on supports high in the air and ask the same people to walk it. Only a few would dare try. Most of the others would have failed, if they had tried.

The point is easily seen. With the plank on the ground one thinks only of walking it. But with the plank high in the air, one thinks of falling. And it is a well-attested fact of life that what we think is usually what will happen. When we give ourselves to God's will, the center of our attention is not ourselves and our weaknesses, but God and His strength. And one who has faith in God cannot think of Him as failing or of being defeated.

Faith gives to one a courageous heart. I was riding with a man the other day in a new car he had just bought. He explained the fine features of the car, and he seemed especially proud of its power. "In fact," he said, "it has an extra, hidden power." Then the car seemed to just leap forward. So sudden was the speed that it threw me back against the seat. He explained that when you press the accelerator against the floor, the motor shifts into the power gear and gives that extra burst of speed.

I thought, that is what happens when a person takes God into his life. He goes along under his normal power, but he knows there is still a greater Power within reach, ready to give him an extra push when it is needed.

We remember that the Psalmist said, "Yea, though I walk through the valley of the shadow of death, I will fear no evil: for Thou art with me . . ." (23:4). Moffatt translates that to read "glen of gloom." It means those difficult, heartbreaking experiences of life, from which we shrink. They may be death, or sickness, or the loss of a job, or many things. But notice that word "through." If we are sure that we will go through, we can stand anything. And the assurance of God's companionship is our assurance of "getting through."

Sometimes we wonder why certain things happen. But as Whittier expressed it:

> Yet in the maddening maze of things
> And tossed by storm and flood,
> To one fixed ground my spirit clings;
> I know that God is good . . .
> —*The Eternal Goodness*

And knowing that, we know that within His will things do eventually work out right. Thus we are not afraid of tomorrow.

YOU GAIN A VICTORY

Regardless of the circumstances of one's life or the difficulties one is called upon to face, I firmly believe God can and will bring any person through to victory, if—and that "if" should be underscored—*if* the person is surrendered to God's will.

A man named Harry wrote his life's story and entitled it *My Wheelchair to the Stars*. You don't usually think of climbing to the stars in a wheelchair, but Harry did. At seven years of age, he had rheumatic fever and later he developed severe arthritis. His pain was such that often even the wearing of clothes was a torture.

His father and mother worked in a textile mill and had no choice but to leave him at home sitting in his wheelchair. As Harry grew older, his illness got into his mind. He began to worry that his life counted for so little. He

47

began to feel there was no reason for living, that he could never be anything except a burden on his parents. He became fearful of what would become of him when they died.

One day he had a particularly bitter experience. He fell out of his chair and lay on the floor helpless for several hours. He said, "I couldn't rise. I struggled and sweated and wept. There on the floor I battled again and again the black wave of bitterness. If I ever prayed, I prayed then. Eventually the postman came. I yelled for him and he came in and picked me up. That postman said, 'Harry, with God all things are possible' " [Mark 10:27].

These words burned themselves into Harry's mind. They drove out the black waves of bitterness. Someone suggested that he paint Christmas cards. He worked six months to make his first card, which would sell for a nickel. But he kept at it, and one year he made $800 from his greeting cards. Then he dared take a reckless plunge. He persuaded his father and mother to mortgage their little home for $2,800. With that, he borrowed $1,000 more to finance a mail order greeting card business. His mother asked, "If you don't sell the cards you have bought, what then?" He simply said, "With God all things are possible." He did sell the cards.

He says he will never forget the first year he did a million dollars worth of business and he said, "I went to the stars in a wheelchair." He ended his story by thanksgiving for his struggles, which God's power had been sufficient to see him through.

Surrender to God's will also gives one a high purpose in life. Our Lord said, ". . . he that loseth his life for my sake shall find it" (Matthew 10:39). Archibald Rutledge told of an old man who ran the engines on a tugboat. The engines were kept spotlessly clean and in the man's face was a radiant glow. In explaining to Mr. Rutledge, he said, "It's this-a-way—I'se got a glory." And having a glory, he had everything.

9.

THE FAITH YOU KEEP
WILL KEEP YOU

THOMAS À KEMPIS expressed one of the fundamental principles of victorious living when he said, "If thou bear the cross, it will soon bear thee." That has been proved again and again. Some time ago, I was in the office of a very successful businessman. It is an elegant office with expensive furnishings, big leather chairs, air-conditioning, and every detail just right. This man has a big business; he is wealthy and highly respected. He has undertaken daring enterprises and has come out on top.

I said, "Tell me the secret of your life." He hesitated for a few moments; he seemed to be lost in some very sacred memory. Then slowly he began to talk about an older brother who was brilliant and good and was great even at the age of twenty-eight when he died. This man was a boy of only fourteen when his brother got sick. The family was too poor to afford a nurse, and it fell to his lot to nurse his brother.

His brother was sick for months, and there were many unpleasant tasks to perform. In the latter stages of his brother's illness, there were times he could hardly bear to do what needed to be done. But he loved his brother, and he carried out those distasteful tasks without complaint. "Always," he said, "when I had done what I could and the task was finished, I felt good about it. After my brother died, I forgot about the unpleasant part of nursing him and I thought about how glad I was I had done it."

Later on this boy grew to manhood, but life did not come easy for him. There were a lot of hard jobs to be done, a lot of times when he wanted to give up and quit.

But day by day, he did his best at the job before him. And then, when he went to bed at night, he felt good inside. He knew he had done what he should have. He learned and practiced one of life's greatest truths: The cross bears those who bear the cross.

Leaving his office, I began thinking of how St. Paul expressed it. He simply said, ". . . I have kept the faith" (II Timothy 4:7). Those words come near the end of probably the last letter the Apostle ever wrote. Soon afterward he was led from his prison cell and executed. He was writing to his young friend, Timothy, telling him to stand firm always, hold true to the course, endure the afflictions.

Now as an old man, St. Paul can look back and see many times when he was tempted to give up, but day by day, through each hard experience, he "kept the faith." Now at the end of the way, though his friends have deserted him, he points out, "Demas hath forsaken me"—"Alexander the coppersmith did me much evil"—"No man stood with me." But in spite of everything, he is serene and not afraid.

He says, "Notwithstanding the Lord stood with me. . . ." (4:17). At the end of the way, when the going is the roughest, we see that the faith he kept, kept him.

A very wise man who had spent his life dealing with people once said to me, "Every person who attained greatness had to fight the temptation of committing suicide." Maybe for most of us the temptation has not been that extreme, but certainly time after time we are tempted to give up and quit. In fact, most of us have at times given up. Not many can look back over all the experiences of life and say with St. Paul, "I have kept the faith."

There have been times when we have not been our best. Of those times we are ashamed. But, thank God, we can also look back upon times when we did "keep the faith." Of those times we are very proud. The victories we have won are now our strongest supports. The faith we kept is keeping us—the crosses we bore are now bearing us.

Max Beerbohm wrote a story called "The Happy Hypocrite." It is about Lord George Hell, who was an unscrupulous villain. Not only was he mean inside, he looked the part outside. Just seeing his face made people afraid of

50

him. He fell in love with a young girl, Little Miss Mere, who was both beautiful and innocent.

She refused him, however, because as she said, "I can never be the wife of a man whose face is not saintly."

Because he wanted her so much, Lord George Hell had the finest maskmaker make him a mask that was saintly. With the mask of a saint, he again sought the love of Miss Mere and won it, and they were married. Day by day he sought to keep up his hypocrisy. He was careful to be unselfish, attentive, and patient. He constantly held in check his evil tendencies in order to appear a saint.

But one day an old enemy found him, and in the presence of his lovely wife, ruthlessly tore off Lord Hell's mask. But when the mask was removed, a saint's face was revealed. He had actually become what he had practiced being day by day. The faith that he had kept, at the last kept him.

Practice keeping faith day by day, and one day you will have enough to keep you.

Look Back and Remember

There are three thoughts to keep in mind, which will help us to keep our faith. The first is: when tempted to give up or lose faith, look back and remember the times you won the victory. Maybe it was some crisis fifteen years ago. You did not see how you could go on, but you did go on and it worked out all right. You discovered new courage and strength inside you that you did not know you had.

Later some other crisis came into your life. You did not see a chance for yourself, but you kept holding on. Maybe some friend helped you that you had not counted on. Anyway, you got through it. Some time later, still another crisis developed. You can't explain it, but as you kept walking through the dark, suddenly you came out into the sunshine. It seemed to work out providentially. As you look back now, you decide it was providential.

We do have unused inner resources; there are friends who help; God does take a hand in our lives. And somehow we eventually come to believe that no matter what life does to us, we can go on. That belief helps us to keep the faith.

FORCES THAT UPHOLD US

St. Paul said, ". . . I have kept the faith," and in the end, the faith that he kept, kept him. But sometimes it seems almost impossible to keep faith. Remembering the past victories we have won will help us to keep from giving up in some new crisis. A second help in keeping the faith is not to forget that, though life has a way of pulling us down, there are even stronger forces in life that hold us up. Life may hurt us, but even more it aids us.

Some years ago, one of the great Sequoia trees in California was cut down. Scientists studied the tree and then told us something of its history. It was a seedling 271 years before Christ was born; 516 years later, it was severely damaged in a forest fire, but nature immediately set to work to repair the damage. Though it was hurt, the tree kept living and growing, and a hundred years later the scar caused by the fire was completely covered. In later years, two other fires damaged the tree, but nature worked to heal those, also.

Life has the power to hurt, to hurt deeply; but life also has the power to heal, to heal completely. When you are tempted to give up your faith, remember that life's helping power is stronger than its hurting power.

FAITH HAS WON FOR OTHERS

A third fact to remember when you are tempted not to keep faith is to remember some of the great triumphs faith has won for others, and also remember you are made of the same stuff of which they were made.

Fix in your mind, for example, Mozart. When he was twenty-five, he went to Vienna. There, ten years later, he died. During those ten years he wrote his matchless music, which will live forever. One day his publisher said to him harshly, "Write, sir, in a more easy and popular style; or I will neither print your music nor pay you a penny for it."

Mozart and his wife were so poor that they often had neither food nor fuel in their tiny house. One cold morning that winter, a friend who came to visit Mozart found his house entirely without heat and the composer and his wife waltzing to keep warm. In fact, the cold and hunger put him in his grave when he was thirty-five.

It must have been an almost unbearable temptation to him to sacrifice his standards. He might so easily have said, "After all, a man has to eat." Or even more easily said, "I cannot see my wife suffer." Instead, he said to his publisher, "Then, my good sir, I have only to resign and die of starvation. I cannot write as you demand." And starve he did; but isn't the world proud of him? The faith he kept is still keeping him.

And when you are tempted not to keep your faith, it will help you to remember that within you is something of what was in Mozart. There is something within every person which, if given a chance, will make that person invincible. That something is God, for God is in us.

10.

FAITH IS THE POWER TO HEAL

As YOU READ the Gospels, you never find an instance when Jesus healed without finding the element of faith somewhere in the story. When the paralytic was brought by his friends and let down through the roof into the presence of Jesus, it was faith. Read it—Mark says, "When Jesus saw their faith . . ." (2:5).

Blind Bartimaeus was sitting by the roadside. He cried out to Christ, and his call was returned. Jesus asked, "What wilt thou that I should do unto thee?" He replied, "Lord, that I might receive my sight." There he is expressing belief not only in the power of Christ to heal but also in Christ's willingness to heal him. He was healed. In explanation, Jesus said, ". . . thy faith hath made thee whole" (Mark 10:46-52).

There was the centurion whose servant was sick. Hearing that Jesus was in the vicinity, he sent word asking that the Lord speak the word that would heal his servant. He believed that Christ did not need even to come to his house. The servant was healed. Jesus said, ". . . I have not found so great faith . . ." (Luke 7:1-10).

There was the cripple at the pool of Bethesda. For thirty-eight years he had been there. He made all manner of excuses about himself. Jesus merely asked one question: "Wilt thou be made whole?" That is, do you really want to be well? Is your mind concerned with the picture of health? His healing was dependent on his own faith (John 5:1-8).

One of the tenderest expressions of faith is seen in the story of the woman who touched the hem of His garment. For twelve years she had been sick. But she wanted so much to be well. Instead of resigning herself to her sickness, all those years she had done all she could to get well. Though she had spent everything she had and nothing had helped her, she would not give up.

She had heard stories of the Man of Galilee who could heal. Not only did she hear, she also believed. She said, "If I may touch but his clothes, I shall be whole." She did touch the hem of his garment, and she was made well. What did Jesus say to her? "Daughter, thy faith hath made thee whole . . ." (Mark 5:25-34).

Immediately following that story is the record of a father who came to Jesus about his daughter. To him Jesus said, "Be not afraid, only believe" (Mark 5:36).

In our conflict between science and superstition, which has been wrongly interpreted as a conflict between science and religion, we came to a day when science raised its flag of victory. But now we are not sure. Perhaps there is no power in wearing a string of amber-colored beads to ward off certain diseases; yet science is coming to realize there was tremendous power in the faith of the person wearing those beads.

How Does Faith Heal?

There are many answers. For one, let us begin with a definition of faith: "Now faith is the substance of things hoped for, the evidence of things not seen" (Hebrews 11:1). In reference to healing, that means that though you are sick, you hope to be well; in spite of your illness, you believe in health. Faith pictures recovery in the sick person's mind. And that is powerful.

The architect gains strength for long, tedious drawing because he pictures in his mind the completed cathedral. Columbus had strength to overcome opposition, to keep on sailing west, in spite of conditions that would have caused almost any person to give up and quit, because in his mind he pictured land ahead.

Before any sick person can ever be well, he must picture health in his mind and believe it can be achieved. That is faith. There is a story of the barber in a small town courting the librarian. For years the folks of the community watched as each afternoon he came by the library to walk home with her. On summer evenings they could be seen sitting together on her porch; in the winter in the parlor.

The town was concerned and felt it would be a good marriage, but the barber could never get quite enough courage to ask the all-important question. Then one day, a dashing, romantic salesman moved into the community. He went one day to borrow a book, and as often happens, he became more interested in the librarian than in the library.

More and more he dropped around to borrow books, and one afternoon the librarian told the barber she would be busy that night. She began being busy a lot of nights. The barber became worried. The entire town began to talk. The barber decided to talk the matter over with his friend, the druggist.

He explained to the druggist how much he loved the girl, that he wanted to marry her, but that his courage failed when it came time to ask her. The druggist explained that he could fix him a capsule that would be just what the barber needed. The capsule was made and the druggist told him that it would act powerfully about fifteen minutes after he took it.

That night he was to see the librarian. He took the capsule as he started to her house and by the time he got there his courage had so developed that he rushed in, grabbed the librarian by the arm and firmly announced, "Come on, we're going to get married." And they did.

A few days later, he said to the druggist, "That was the most powerful capsule I ever took. What was in it?" The druggist smiled and quietly replied, "Three things—first, a gelatin capsule; second, some sugar; third, the belief that you could do it."

The third ingredient was the one that mattered. Belief or faith is usually the ingredient that makes the difference between success and failure—between being well and being sick.

A college friend of mine, Dr. Carl J. Sanders, now a distinguished pastor in Virginia, tells of one of his members who was carried into the operating room in a Richmond hospital for surgery. As they were preparing to give him the anesthesia, the patient turned to the doctor and nervously asked, "Doctor, do you think I will die on the operating table?"

"Indeed I do not. Why?" demanded the doctor.

"I just can't get over the feeling that I am going to die during the operation," the patient insisted.

The doctor ordered the patient taken back to his room. He had his pastor, Dr. Sanders, called and that afternoon the patient and the pastor were alone together. They talked about God and about faith. The next morning the patient was again carried to the operating room, but now he carried faith with him and the surgeon had no hesitation in going on with the operation.

The point being: science at its best is now realizing that without faith it is insufficient.

Admiral Du Pont was explaining to Admiral Farragut the reasons why he had failed to enter Charleston Harbor with his fleet of ironclads. Farragut listened until he was through, and then said, "Du Pont, there is one reason more."

"What is that?" questioned Du Pont.

"You did not believe you could."

On one occasion it was even said of Jesus that He could do no mighty works because of the unbelief of the people. It was in His own home town. "Is not this the carpenter's son?" (Matthew 13:55) they said with contempt. They knew His brothers and sisters. They recognized Him only as an ordinary person among them. And because they had no faith in Him, they failed to experience His miracle-working power (Matthew 13:54-58).

If you do not believe in the power of Christ to heal, it is certain that you will never experience His power. The Bible tells us that: "But without faith it is impossible to please him: for he that cometh to God must believe that he is, and that he is a rewarder of them that diligently seek him" (Hebrews 11:6).

Mussolini made a sorry mess of his life but at least he expressed one great truth. He said: "The capacity of modern man to believe is unbelievable."

The extent to which you can believe if you will only let yourself will amaze you. Perhaps your faith is small, but Christ is *not* small. And remember: It is not a perfect faith that heals—it is a perfect Saviour who heals. But He needs what faith you have.

FAITH CREATES A PICTURE OF HEALTH

Faith creates a mental picture of health, and without a healthy attitude of mind, nobody can be healthy. As Leslie Weatherhead put it: "Sometimes it is more important to know what kind of a fellah has a germ, than what kind of a germ has a fellah."

There are germs and sickening circumstances in every life. But inner faith is stronger than outward circumstances. As Dr. Harry Emerson Fosdick said it: "Fear imprisons, faith liberates; fear paralyzes, faith empowers; fear disheartens, faith encourages; and most of all, fear puts hopelessness into the heart of life, while faith rejoices in its God."

Faith begins where physical resources leave off. Annie Johnson Flint says it well:

57

When we have exhausted our store of endurance,
When our strength has failed ere the day is half done,
When we reach the end of our hoarded resources,
Our Father's full giving is only begun.
                                    —*He Giveth More*

Louis Binstock tells a marvelous story of the power of faith. A little girl living on the Gaspe Peninsula in Quebec had contracted a rare disease which only rest, time, and the will to live could cure. But the child was so enamored of the statue of Saint Anne she could see from her window that she made no effort to recover. Death, she felt, would unite her with her saintly friend.

Desiring to die, she became weaker every day. To the priest she said, "If the Saint does not wish me to die, she will give me some sign."

A few nights later the little girl was awakened by the sound of glorious organ music. She looked through the window and saw the statue of Saint Anne radiantly transfused in silvery light. "That is the sign!" she exclaimed. "The Saint wants me to live." Immediately she began to get well. The people of the town became excited over the wonderful miracle.

The priest called the people together and told them how it had actually happened. The sign had been arranged. Knowing how the full moon always bathed the statue of Saint Anne, he had slipped into the church to play the organ at the right moment and had awakened the child.

The people were resentful. They did not want to give up their miracle. To them the priest said, "I know how you feel. But some day you will understand you have beheld a far greater miracle." Instead of the organ music and the lighted statue, something that could be explained merely by a full moon and an organist playing, they had seen the miracle of the power of faith within that sick little girl.

Jesus still walks through the crowds. But only those with a deep hunger for healing, those who with deep sincerity reach out by faith to Him, ever hear Him saying, ". . . thy faith hath made thee whole; go in peace . . ." (Mark 5:34).

11.

MIRACLE DRUGS FOR THE SOUL

RECENTLY a close friend of mine was granted $65,000 for research to seek to discover new medicines for mental illnesses. I shall enjoy discussing with him his work and watching his progress. During the past several years, I have been fascinated by the remarkable progress being made in the treatment of mental diseases.

A short generation ago, when the word "health" was mentioned, we thought only of physical health. As far as the mind was concerned, there were only two kinds of people—the sane and the insane. The treatment for the insane was to put them away where they would not be dangerous. Now we are realizing that there are degrees of mental illness and that often such an illness can be successfully treated and cured.

In recent years much has been learned about emotional illness. We now know that a person may be healthy physically and mentally and yet be ill emotionally. Some emotional illnesses are of such an extent that one cannot live normally or happily. Medical science is giving increased attention to mental and emotional diseases. Much research is being done in these fields; there are an increasingly large number of physicians who are exclusively treating people who are healthy physically but sick in other ways.

We are also realizing that there is another area of sickness. One might be physically, mentally, and emotionally normal but be spiritually sick. Not only are ministers giving much attention to the area of spiritual health, but also this subject is discussed among many physicians and those who are doing scientific research. In fact, many of us believe that spiritual health is the basis of all health.

Some time ago, I wrote a book on the miracles of Christ, the title of which is *The Touch of the Master's Hand*. As I restudied the Lord's miracles, I was amazed at how many of them resulted from spiritual healing. For example, there was the paralyzed man who was let down through the roof (Mark 2:1-12). This man could not walk; he was a physical invalid. But Christ saw beyond his physical illness and saw it was caused by his spiritual illness. So Jesus said, "Son, thy sins be forgiven thee." Through spiritual healing, the man also received physical healing.

Recently I was in another city to preach for five nights. While there I had dinner in the homes of three physicians. These men talked of their work and each mentioned the great value of many new miracle drugs. Diseases that once meant almost certain death can now be healed surely and quickly. As these physicians spoke of how much easier and more effective their work now is with the wonderful new medicines, I found myself wishing I had some miracle drugs for the soul. I thought of such very different things as hatred and sorrow, pride and fear, guilt and indifference. Then I realized we do have drugs that can cure the soul.

Today we are delighted to have miracle drugs for physical, mental and emotional illnesses. But the worst sickness is spiritual sickness. We have cures for that, too. Let me list some cures for soul-sickness.

(1) One is *humility*. Study Jesus' dealings with spiritually sick people and you will see that never could He do anything with a proud man. On one occasion a young man came to Jesus asking, ". . . what good thing shall I do, that I may have eternal life?" (Matthew 19:16). I don't think he was asking how he might get to heaven. Rather, I think he was seeking to possess real life as he had seen it in Jesus. I have heard people say, "I'm not really living." That is how that man felt.

This man said that he had lived a good, moral life but he had missed something that he wanted. Jesus knew of this man's possessions and the pride he had in them. So he told him to give what he had away and then follow Him. Jesus never objected to a man's wealth, except when that wealth gave him a false sense of security and importance.

St. Augustine, in *The City of God*, said that the world

has been controlled by two parties: Those who have governed by "love of self to the point of contempt of God" and those who have governed by "love of God to the point of contempt of self."

It has been well said that humility is not thinking poorly of yourself. Humility is not thinking of yourself at all.

Sometimes God has a way of putting us on our knees. I have seen some hard experiences come into the lives of people, but I am convinced that anything that makes us humble is a blessing. We have so much today—lots of money, fine cars and houses and clothes, plenty to eat—it is mighty hard to be humble. But when one is sick in spirit, if he can lose himself in dedication, his sickness will be healed.

(2) Another miracle drug for the sick soul is *truth*. I mean the acceptance of the truth about ourselves. That is not easy. When Ralph Barton, one of the most popular of American cartoonists, took his own life, he left this message: "I have run from wife to wife, from house to house, and from country to country in a ridiculous effort to escape from myself. In doing so I am very much afraid I have caused a great deal of unhappiness to those who have loved me . . . No one is responsible for this . . . except myself . . . I've done it because I am fed up with inventing devices for getting through twenty-four hours every day."

When a person has been caught in the clutches of liquor, the hardest step for him to take on the road to recovery is to admit to himself that he needs help. That is true of any sin or sickness. The Bible promises that God will forgive our sins, but first we must confess them—face up to the horrible fact that we have sinned.

I have spent much time counseling with soul-sick people. It is a hard job to get them to take off their masks of pretense. Facing the truth about yourself will work miracles of healing.

(3) *Forgiveness* is a cure for the soul. Forgiveness has two handles—one that we must take hold of for ourselves and one that we must offer to certain other people. Read the four Gospels, and you are impressed with how often Jesus said to a soul-sick person words such as, "Thy sins be forgiven thee," "Neither do I condemn thee, go and sin no

61

more." Jesus died on a cross that we might have forgiveness. But in order to receive healing power, we must have faith that God will forgive, must repent of our sin, must have faith that God has forgiven. There are many people who are receiving treatment for physical, mental, or emotional illness who are not being cured. Their trouble is deeper. On their heart is the burden of some guilt. There is only one cure and that is the forgiveness of God.

Also, we must forgive. Ill feelings toward any other person will make the one who holds those feelings ill.

(4) Another miracle drug for the soul is *service*. When a person becomes wrapped up in himself, he gets sick in his soul. Everyone has heard the prayer of the old man who prayed:"Lord, bless me and my wife, My son John and his wife, Us four and no more." Farther down the street there lived a couple without children who prayed: "Lord, bless us two, And that will do." Around the corner there lived an old bachelor whose prayer was, "Lord, bless only me, That's as far as I can see."

We remember that our Lord said, "He that findeth his life shall lose it: and he that loseth his life for my sake shall find it" (Matthew 10:39). You never become spiritually whole until you find something to give yourself for.

(5) For the soul that is sick, the finest healing agent is *the Presence of God*. I have seen people try all sorts of things to find spiritual healing and fail. I have even seen the things I have mentioned fail—forgetting self, honestly facing the truth about ourselves, forgiveness both received and given, and unselfish service. They are wonderful healing agents, but no medicine heals in every case. Penicillin does not heal every time.

But there is one cure that never fails. When one honestly seeks the Presence of God and finds Him, he is healed. The Psalmist said:

Bless the LORD, O my soul, and forget not all his benefits: Who forgiveth all thine iniquities; who healeth all thy diseases.

(Psalm 103:2, 3)

12.

PENICILLIN FOR DESPAIR

ABBE PIERRE has a phrase—"penicillin for despair." He declares that to be the world's greatest need. I am inclined to agree. Every person who has been plagued by anxious fears feels the need of "penicillin for despair." Certainly Christ felt that need.

As He knelt that night in Gethsemane, the Bible says, he ". . . began to be sore amazed and very heavy" (Mark 14:33). The Revised Version translates that to read, He ". . . began to be greatly amazed and sore troubled." Moffatt's translation gives, ". . . he began to feel appalled and agitated."

Vincent Taylor, the world-famous Greek scholar, says, "Those verbs denote distress which follows a great shock." He points out that hundreds and thousands of British people are still suffering from the shock of the last war, though many of them do not realize it. Likewise, there are many in America who are still suffering from the shock of that war. And there are numerous other shocks that have come into the personal lives of people.

I have had many people talk to me about how they went to bed only to toss and turn for hours before sleep would come; others of how they suddenly began to tremble, or break into a cold sweat, or feel constant fatigue, or have an abnormal dryness in the mouth, or a palpitating heart, or a constant headache, or a deadness of feeling when they seemed to lose ability to love their own family, even God. Some have even told me about inclinations to suicide.

For people who know the sufferings brought by anxious fears, I have deep sympathy. I have had some of those same feelings. Nearly every normal person has at some time been very heavy—greatly distressed—troubled—appalled—agitated. Some people seem condemned to live with an anxiety neurosis as a constant companion.

In times of anxious strain we are told to "have faith" and all our troubles will magically disappear. That is simply not true. Jesus had faith, but He also knew the meaning of naked terror. Some of the greatest saints have cried out for a "penicillin for despair," yet they also had faith.

We are told that our fears are imaginary. That is a misstatement. All fears are real—none are imaginary. It may be that imagination caused our fears, or it may be that we reacted in the wrong way to some circumstance of life, but the fears themselves are not imaginary.

We are told to "pull ourselves together," but we are not sure what that means. Many do not feel they have strength enough to pull even if they knew what to pull on.

When we have infections of certain types, the physician gives us penicillin and soon the infection is gone.

When you feel despair, or deep anxiety, or trembling fear, or nervous strain, what attitude should you take toward it? Examine the experience of Christ when He felt "very heavy." You will find it in Mark 14:32-36.

We know that Christ was God and that as God He had supernatural insight and power. But also Christ was man, and as man He experienced our same hungers and thirsts. He endured temptation that was real. He had human desires. Also, He had experiences of deep anxiety and despair.

Thus we know that anxious fears may come even though one does have faith. We should not feel ashamed because of nervous symptoms. These experiences come to nearly everyone. But there is such a thing as "penicillin for despair." It isn't a pill or a shot in the arm; it is an action or a series of actions. In His moment of despair, Christ did these three things:

HE GOT ALONE

That night in Gethsemane He moved a distance from the crowd and took with Him His three closest friends. There are times when it is good for us to be with crowds. There are other times when we need to be with some trusted and close friends. Jesus, no doubt, talked with these three about His troubles. Often that helps. It is wonderful to have a friend to share our deepest thoughts. Often it helps to talk with a minister or a competent counselor. But then Jesus went further alone. It is important to see this.

When one is in some dark valley, his first impulse is to tell his troubles to every person who will listen. The reason we want to tell our troubles is because we want sympathy; we get soothing satisfaction from the pity of others and from self-pity. We deny this, but it is true.

The more we talk about our troubles, the worse they become. Speech has a much greater effect on the emotions than thinking has. We can talk ourselves into almost anything, and the more we talk our troubles, the worse they become. Jesus got alone.

He Looked to God

"And he said, Abba, Father, all things are possible unto thee . . ." (Mark 14:36). He took His mind off Himself, and that does much to relieve one of anxiety and fear. But it is hard to do because part of the mind wants to hold onto its worries and despair. That is the easiest way out. To despair is to lose hope, and to lose hope is to be able to give up and quit.

Frequently we translate our despair into bodily illness. Maybe we don't become invalids, but we never "feel well." Much of the sickness of people is merely an escape from reality, the easiest way out. But this is never a final solution. Deep down we are ashamed of our cowardice. We feel guilty for selling our courage to buy sympathy.

When one looks into the face of God, he has hope because he does know that "all things are possible unto" Him.

When Jesus "began to be sore amazed and very heavy" —distressed, troubled, and despairing, He did three things: He got alone; He looked into the face of God; and

In the midst of despair, the great temptation is to retire, to slip into illness, to surrender. It is a great struggle to do something. It was a struggle for our Lord. Luke vividly portrays the strain Christ was under. He says, ". . . his sweat was as it were great drops of blood falling down to the ground" (Luke 22:44). But in spite of the struggle, Jesus centered His mind on something to do. He refused to retire into Himself.

Activity is often the best cure for the blues. Physicians tell us that our fear thoughts come from the higher brain centers while physical activity comes from the lower brain centers. When one begins to exercise those lower brain centers through activity, it lessens the tension of the upper brain centers. I have read of operations by which certain parts of the brain are removed to lessen those fear thoughts. I knew of a man who took daily exercise. He said it "straightened out his thoughts."

What did Jesus do? He prayed, "not my will, but thine, be done." He committed Himself wholly to the will of God. There is the faith that is the answer to fear. It lifts one's thoughts away from his own troubles and centers his mind on the strength of God.

It has been truly said, "In His will is our peace." That is the "penicillin for despair." Commitment to His will cures despair and brings peace for several reasons: it takes from us the fear of getting lost; it relieves us of the burden of the responsibility of tomorrow; it gives us the approval of a good conscience; it gives us a constructive life to live. Dedication to His will enables us to say with the Psalmist, "Yea, though I walk through the valley of the shadow of death, I will fear no evil: for thou art with me . . ." (23:4). Realizing that He is with us, we have confidence that we will get through even the worst experience. Thus there is no room in our minds for despair.

13.

DON'T LET YOUR DEFEATS DEFEAT YOU

IN MANY WAYS the minister must learn to say to people, "Don't let your defeats defeat you." I read the many letters that come, but none of them ever say, "This has been such a happy day in my life, I wanted to write you about it."

No one ever phones to say, "My marriage is so perfect I called to tell you about it." Nobody ever comes by to say, "God has so abundantly blessed me that I have more money than I can spend." No—the minister hears about the heartaches, the broken dreams, the poverty, the disappointments.

It seems that everybody is in some way defeated in life and, as a matter of fact, everybody is. Some have much harder defeats than do others—but along the way every person meets a defeat. In his book, *The Christ of the Round Table,* E. Stanley Jones tells about a man standing to say during a discussion, "For me Christianity means victory—victory—victory." But quickly another rose and stated, "For me it means victory—defeat—victory." Then a third added, "For me it means defeat—victory—defeat."

Surely most of us would confess that life is not a series of unbroken victories. Generously mixed in with our triumphs are many defeats. Sometimes we fail when we have done our very best; sometimes we fail because we didn't do our best.

Several months ago, I was preaching in another city. In the audience was a minister whom I consider one of the greatest in America. He has a great mind and a deep consecration. After the meeting he came up and suggested we slip out together for a cup of coffee and a visit. I was delighted and honored to be in his presence. He is the kind of a minister I would like to be.

In a quiet corner of the little restaurant, we talked of many things, but eventually began to confess our faults to each other. That is a dangerous thing to do. You know the story of the three ministers who were traveling together and decided to confess their faults to each other. One named his faults, the second named his, and they were both pretty bad. They turned to the third who until then had been silent. He said, "My worst fault is gossiping, and I can't wait until I get back home."

But this minister told me of the struggles he has had to control his emotions of fear and anger. Sometimes he feels an overwhelming fear just before he is to speak. It is a burden to him. Sometimes he has great difficulty controlling his anger. He told me that we needed to invent an "ecclesiastical profanity," so that he could express himself at times. Of course, he was partly joking.

Then very seriously he said, "Only Christ perfectly mastered life. Even the best Christians among us have pagan intervals." By that he meant, no one is perfectly good. We all have defeats, but defeats can be blessings.

One of my favorite books in the Bible is Hebrews. It was written to a small band of people who were discouraged. They had been converted from one religious group to Christianity. When they left their own group, their old friends and even their own families had turned against them! They found it hard to make a living and they faced bitter persecution.

The Book of Hebrews contains the most eloquent statement on faith ever recorded anywhere. It is the eleventh chapter, which begins, "Now faith is the substance of things hoped for, the evidence of things not seen." That chapter goes on to tell of the struggles of great people in history and how, by faith, they won mighty victories. To these people the writer is saying, hold onto your faith and you will not be finally defeated.

The next chapter begins by telling them how they can hold their faith—by remembering those who gained victories, by turning away from that besetting sin, by being patient day by day, but mainly by, "Looking unto Jesus the author and finisher of our faith. . . ." Now notice the next words about Jesus. "Who was the greatest teacher of all time"—no, that is not what it says. "Who had the power to perform mighty miracles"—no, that is not mentioned. This is what it says: ". . . who for the joy that was set before him endured the cross. . . ." He knew the meaning of deep suffering and sorrow.

Then we read in the twelfth chapter these words: "My son, despise not thou the chastening of the Lord. . . . For whom the Lord loveth he chasteneth. . . ." Sometimes God puts us on our backs in order to make us look up. Sometimes it is just the circumstances of life that bring our disappointing defeats. But remember, don't let your defeats defeat you.

BE RECEPTIVE

Defeats can bless you because they make you more receptive to God.

The Book of Hebrews tells us, "By faith Moses . . . endured, as seeing him who is invisible" (11:23, 27). Where did Moses get that faith? It came out of his defeat. Once he lost his temper and did wrong. As a result, he became a fugitive. At the age of forty, he was a penniless, broken failure. He had lived in a palace, but now he had to take a job as a sheepherder.

Out on the range one day, he saw a bush on fire. It was strange because the bush never burned up. He went to investigate and there he heard the voice of God. He listened to God and obeyed, and he went on to great victories. Had it not been for the chastening of a defeat, he would never have heard and responded to God.

After World War II, we sent teachers to Japan to help rebuild the country. One of those teachers remarked, "It is so much easier to teach a defeated country because it knows its methods must have been wrong. A victorious country is prone to feel it has been right and does not care to learn new things."

Sometimes we have to be defeated before we listen to God.

A famous golf champion said that he learned from his defeats, never from his victories. After he had been defeated in a tournament, he would go to some golf teacher and say, "Tell me what I am doing wrong." Then he would work to correct his mistakes.

Likewise when defeats come in life, we are more prone to come to God for correction and instruction. Maurice Maeterlinck said, "Beauty and grandeur are all about us but only when some emergency or disaster cracks the shell of life do we grope our way upward to catch the gleams which come through the cracks."

Be Resourceful

If we refuse to be defeated by our defeats, they will make us more resourceful. Booker T. Washington spoke of the "advantage of a disadvantage." He himself was an example. He was born a slave, and one of his jobs was to carry the books of the white children to school. He had no books of his own, and he was not permitted inside the school. But he developed a passion for education and he later became one of the best-educated men of his day. He devoted his life to making an education possible for those of his race.

Often when we have failed in some way, we realize our own strengths are not sufficient. Then we discover the resources and strengths of the spiritual. We recall the name of Joseph Goebbels, who was Hitler's chief assistant. In his diary he made several references to Ghandi and each time refers to him as a fool and a fanatic. But through physical force, Goebbels failed; through spiritual power, Gandhi won his life's victory.

Sometimes we must fail before we are willing to discover our spiritual resources.

Become Redemptive

Not only do our defeats make us more receptive and

more resourceful; what is more important, they make us more redemptive.

Who is the most beloved American of all time? His mother died when he was a baby. He had very little opportunity to go to school and to prepare himself. He ran for the legislature but was defeated. He entered business but a worthless partner put him into bankruptcy. He loved a girl dearly, but she died. Later he married another, but it was an unhappy marriage.

He served one term in Congress but was defeated for reelection. He worked for an appointment to the United States Land Office but did not get it. He tried to be a lyceum lecturer but failed. He ran for the Senate but was defeated. He ran for the office of Vice-President but was defeated. His name is Abraham Lincoln. He "endured chastening," and who can deny that he became a true son of God?

I read of a shepherd who broke the leg of a wayward lamb. Through nursing it back to health, the shepherd knew he would win the lamb to obedience to his voice. And through our defeats, God often nurses us to obedience to Him.

14.

POWER TO DESTROY THE EVIL WITH WHICH YOU LIVE

FUTURE HISTORIANS will probably describe the time in which we are now living as the age of power. We have seen the beginning of the use of atomic power, the development of electric power, and mechanical engines with tremendous power. And now we are learning to utilize power drawn from the rays of the sun. Today man has at his disposal unmeasured power.

Our generation is also making great progress in the field of spiritual and personal power. Some of the best thinkers in the world today are studying the individual man, his weaknesses and needs, his sources of inner strength and power. And we are beginning to develop a clearer understanding of Christ and what He taught than the world has ever had before.

For example, today we are looking at Luke 10:19 with new light and understanding. Jesus said: "Behold, I give unto you power to tread on serpents and scorpions, and over all the power of the enemy; and nothing shall by any means hurt you." That verse has been misunderstood by certain ignorant and fanatical people, and they have developed a religious sect called "snake-handlers." This practice is so repulsive to normal people that we have looked away from that verse and wished it were not in the Bible. Actually it is one of the most wonderful promises our Lord gave to us.

When Jesus said "serpents and scorpions," He was speaking in parables, referring to those sinister, slimy things that slither through your life—the things that strike you down and poison your very soul. Please pardon me for even mentioning the idea, but if you were forced to live in a house in which you knew there was a snake, you would never have an easy moment. That very thought causes us to cringe. Yet, that is a picture of many lives. They are forced to live with some sinister weakness that sets up constant dread in their minds.

I have come to know many people who must live with some serpent. There is the one with a suicidal tendency always lurking in the shadows. In moments of stress and strain it strikes, sometimes with fatal consequences. One of the most pitiful people in our society is the sex pervert. We normally have contempt for homosexuals, yet for some of those people it is an awful burden to bear. There is the alcoholic who goes along for weeks and sometimes even years, and then suddenly in an unguarded moment the thing strikes.

People live with other serpents, such as deep feelings of inadequacy and inferiority. Others live with abnormal fears that cause them to break out in cold sweats. Some are extremely sensitive to criticism. The other day I saw a group of children afflicted with cerebral palsy. They lack muscular control. I know people who seem to lack emotional control. In many lives there is hate and prejudice.

But Jesus promised power over all these "serpents and scorpions." Instead of being hurt by them, we can overcome and destroy them.

THE ARMOR OF THE SPIRIT

Jesus promises us power over the weaknesses and sinister enemies of our lives and says, ". . . nothing shall by any means hurt you."

That does not mean that all your weaknesses will suddenly be taken away. It does not mean that you will not get some injury from life, that you will not experience disappointment, that you will not get sick or grow old. But it does mean that you can have the kind of power that is stronger than those things. You can be clad in an armor, not of steel, but an armor of the spirit, and the enemies of life cannot break through to really hurt you. With the power of Christ, you will not be destroyed or dethroned from the mastery of your life.

In connection with this power over life's enemies, Christ also promises power to gain thrilling victories in the conquests of life. Speaking to His disciples, Christ said, "But ye shall receive power, after that the Holy Ghost is come upon you . . ." (Acts 1:8). He was speaking to very ordinary men, men with all the human weaknesses that people have today. But Jesus is saying, "You men will become endowed with extraordinary power so that you can accomplish things you never dreamed of accomplishing before— you can even conquer the world."

The story of how those men did go out and "turn the world upside down" is well known. They became irresistible. So it has continued through the years. For example, in the little city of Assisi, there lived a gay youth by the name of Francis. He lived for pleasure and the satisfaction of his physical appetites. Francis was not satisfied with himself, but he seemed unable to change his ways.

73

One day he attended a little church. He came as most people come to church, not expecting anything to happen. The priest was reading some passage of the Scripture, when the miracle happened. The cold print of the Bible suddenly began to live for Francis. The life leaped from the printed page into his heart, and he became a transformed person. He began to preach with such winsome beauty and effectiveness that he transformed the life of his day. What happened? He became the possessor of a mighty spiritual power.

A story is told about an old preacher who visited Aldersgate Street Church in London. He knew it was the church where John Wesley had received that marvelous experience through which his heart had become "strangely warmed." He knew how Wesley had gone out from there, the possessor of a power so warm and yet so strong that through his preaching the moral tone of all England was changed and a worldwide revival was begun.

This devout old preacher asked the exact spot in the church where Wesley had been sitting when it happened. Reverently he sat down, lifted up his eyes and fervently prayed, "O Lord, do it again—do it again." And to this very hour, God is doing it again for those who really want to receive His Power.

How You Can Get This Power

"Behold, I give you power," Christ said. Again he promised, "ye shall receive power." And His promises hold good for any person today just as they did for those to whom He first spoke those words.

If you want the power of Christ in your life—power to overcome those things that hurt you and power to give you victory in life—how can you get it? All power is channeled to us through mechanisms. Man learned how to build electric generators and thereby made electric power available. The scientists gave us the formula for atomic power, and we build the plants to produce it.

And the mechanism through which man receives the power of God is the experience we call conversion. We remember that one night a man by the name of Nicodemus came to Jesus. He said to Christ, ". . . no man can do these miracles that thou doest, except God be with him" (John 3:2). Nicodemus recognized in Christ the power of God. He was asking how he, too, might have that power.

Jesus said, ". . . ye must be born again" (3:7). That is, you must become a different person. But how can that be accomplished? Nicodemus asked. Jesus did not explain. Instead, he pointed out that the wind blows but we do not know where it comes from or where it goes. Yet we know it blows. Likewise, the Spirit of God comes into our lives, but we cannot explain exactly how that happens.

Then Jesus spoke the most marvelous word this world has ever heard: "For God so loved the world, that he gave his only begotten Son, that whosoever believeth in him should not perish, but have everlasting life" (John 3:16).

There are those who admit, "I do need to change," and they set in to change themselves. They quit this and they quit that. They resolve to do this and to do that. But they find that their self-improvement programs just do not work. But when by faith they believe in Christ and accept Him as their Saviour, the miracle happens. As a result of yielding ourselves to Christ two things happen:

(1) We turn loose of those things in our lives that are wrong. We realize that evil in our lives blocks out the power of God, and we are led to turn from our wicked ways. Remember, when you take hold of Christ, you turn loose of the wrong you have been doing. To surrender to Christ also means to surrender those things that are not according to His Spirit.

(2) When you accept Christ, His will becomes your will and in all things and in every situation you say, "What would Christ do?" As best you understand it, you seek to live as He would live if He were in your place. You pray as He prayed: ". . . nevertheless not my will, but thine, be done" (Luke 22:42). With the surrendering of your evil ways and of your life to the will of God, there begins to flow into your life the power of God.

15.

CHANGE YOUR THOUGHTS AND YOU CHANGE YOURSELF

MOST PEOPLE would like to change something in their lives. Some people would like to change almost everything in their lives. The Bible teaches us that to change what we want to change, we must change our thoughts. To see this truth, we need to understand three great Bible texts.

The first one: "For as he thinketh in his heart, so is he" (Proverbs 23:7). Down through the centuries wise men have said this same thing. Marcus Aurelius has been called the wisest man of the Roman Empire. He said, "Your life is what your thoughts make of it." One of the wisest men who ever lived in America was Ralph Waldo Emerson, who said, "A man is what he thinks about all day long."

Though this principle has been proved through centuries of experience, still multitudes have not yet seen it. We have the idea that our lives are determined not by what we think but rather by what we have. If we could just make more money and buy all the things we want, we think we would have everything necessary to bring happiness and contentment into our lives. So, we expend our energies to possess things; and even if we are successful, we still end up the same frustrated, unhappy people.

Dr. Norman Vincent Peale tells a wonderful story. A barber's supply association was having a convention. Their publicity agent went into the worst section of the city and found the most unpromising specimen of human nature there—a dirty, unshaven, ragged, drunken, sad man. The barbers went to work on him; he was given a bath, haircut, shave, shampoo, facial massage, manicure—the works.

Then he was dressed in fine clothes from top to bottom,

fitted by the best tailor. They put a handkerchief, folded just right, in his coat pocket, put on him neat shoes and a proper hat. They provided a smart-looking topcoat and even put a cane in his hand. They photographed each step of this transformation and had the pictures printed in the newspaper. The people were amazed at the change the barbers wrought. He was transformed from a bum in the gutter to one of the finest-looking gentlemen in the city.

One man was so impressed that he offered the man a good job. He was to come to work the next morning at eight o'clock. But he was late. In fact, he didn't show up all day. So the employer went looking for him and he found him down in the same old street, dead drunk, sleeping on some old newspapers in an alley. His fine clothes were rumpled and soiled. The end of the story is, though you may change a person's outside appearance, the man himself remains the same until he is changed inside.

We sometimes think that our lives are determined by the circumstances that surround us. Actually, the opposite is true. The kind of person you are determines the circumstances about you. If you want a better life, the place to change is inside yourself.

THE RENEWING OF YOUR MIND

The way to change your life is to change your thoughts. St. Paul said it better. He said. ". . . be ye transformed by the renewing of your mind . . ." (Romans 12:2). We make a great mistake when we belittle the power of our thoughts. God gave man a marvelous body, but the most wonderful thing man possesses is his brain.

A scientist once stated: "If you took all the electronic equipment in the United States and put it all together, you would not have as complicated a machine as is one human brain." In California, I had dinner one night with a man who helps build these great computers. He told me that in a matter of seconds, he could work out a problem that would take eighty scientists a lifetime to solve.

On the other hand, a computer lacks the power of

thought. It can only work out in a mechanical way the thoughts of some human brain. And no machine can know the thrill of romance, of happy memories, of inspired imagination, and of a deep spiritual experience. But there is this valid comparison—put a human thought into that machine and it will give a certain answer. Put in a different thought and you get a different answer. So it is with life. Your thought determines your answer.

Let me give a simple illustration. One Sunday morning as I was driving to church, I saw the fine building of another church, and many people going in there. On down at the next corner, many, many more people were going into another great church. I noticed a throng of people headed for still another church across the street.

As I drove along, several cars passed me that gave evidence of being in a great hurry. I reasoned they were going to church and they were hurrying to get a seat. I found myself getting a little uneasy. I began to think, everybody is going to these other churches and there will be nobody coming to my church. Then I began to think up some criticisms of those other preachers. I am ashamed to admit it, but human nature works that way, even among preachers.

Then I caught myself. "This is silly for me to think like this, and it isn't my normal way of thinking." Then I started to think of those other ministers and the great work for Christ they are doing. I thought of the loyalty and consecration of the members of those other churches. I began praying that God would especially bless the work of those other men, and I thought of many other ministers of the city.

Then the words of Hebrews 12:1 came to mind: "Wherefore seeing we also are compassed about with so great a cloud of witnesses, let us lay aside every weight. . . ." Instead of becoming jealous, I began to feel more confidence and joy and I was glad that the Lord's work is being carried on by so many people. My entire spirit was changed just because I changed the way I looked at the situation. And not only did I also have a large congregation to preach to, the people said I preached better that day.

The outcome doesn't depend on the situation you face; it depends on how you think about it.

His Mind in You

"For as he thinketh in his heart, so is he." What you think is what you are. "Be ye transformed by the renewing of your mind." You change your life by changing your thoughts. The final step in this process is: "Let this mind be in you, which was also in Christ Jesus" (Philippians 2:5).

One of the greatest stories ever written is "The Great Stone Face," by Nathaniel Hawthorne. On the side of the mountain was the face. It was strong, kind, and honorable. Living nearby was a boy by the name of Ernest. Day by day he would look at that face, and he was thrilled by what he saw. Through his boyhood and even after he became a man, Ernest spent many hours gazing upon the face on the mountain.

There was a legend that someday a man would appear in the community who would look exactly like the face. For years that legend had persisted. One day, when the people were discussing the legend, someone suddenly cried out, "Behold, behold, Ernest is himself the likeness of the Great Stone Face." Indeed he was; he had become like his thoughts.

The secret desires of our hearts eventually show up in our very appearance. Once someone wanted Lincoln to meet a certain man. "I do not want to see him," Lincoln said. But his friend protested, "You do not even know him." Lincoln replied, "I do not like his face." "A man cannot be held responsible for his face," the friend said. "Any grown man is responsible for the look on his face," the President insisted. And Lincoln was right. His own face was an example. Although it was homely and rough, in Lincoln's face one sees the very principles of sympathy and honesty that made him the greatest of all Americans.

Some psychologists have made extensive studies, which show that a person's thoughts show up in his features. I have noticed that married couples who have lived together happily and harmoniously over a number of years come to look more like brother and sister than like husband and wife. As they live together, enjoy common experiences, think alike, they tend to look alike.

I have a dear friend. Whenever I am in his presence I feel strangely different. It seems as though Christ is there, too. A man once wrote to Phillips Brooks, "When I hear you preach I somehow forget about you because you make me think of Christ." This friend does that for me. As I have come to know him better, I have learned his secrets.

Through the years, he has read regularly some portion of Matthew, Mark, Luke, or John—the books that tell about Christ. As he reads those stories he pictures himself as present when they happened. He thinks of himself as a personal friend of the Master. Through repeated reading he has become familiar with every detail of Christ's life. He has come to know Christ better than he knows any other man, and he thinks of Christ as being with him at all times.

Whenever he has a decision to make he first asks, "What would Jesus do?" And whatever he believes the answer to that question is, he does just that as best he can. Little by little, the mind of Christ has taken possession of his mind; and as that has happened, his actions and his life have become like Christ.

If you would like to have inner peace and personal power in your life, put before yourself the One who can give it to you. You will be amazed at the change in you when His mind becomes your mind—when you change your thoughts to His thoughts.

16.

THE MAGIC OF BELIEVING

CLAUDE M. BRISTOL asks: "Is there a something, a force, a factor, a power, a science—call it what you will—which a few people understand and use to overcome their difficulties and achieve outstanding success?"

As a newspaper reporter, he studied the religions of the world and watched them operate. In hospitals he saw people die while others who were just as sick got well. He watched football teams win while other teams who had just as good material lost. He studied the lives of the great men and women in all lines of human endeavor. As a result of years of study, he wrote a book on *The Magic of Believing,* in which he says:

> Gradually I discovered that there is a golden thread that runs through all the teachings and makes them work for those who sincerely accept and apply them, and that thread can be named in a single word—belief. It is the same element or factor, belief, which causes people to be cured through mental healing, enables others to climb high the ladder of success . . . there's genuine magic in believing.

Long before Bristol wrote his book, William James, the great psychologist, arrived at the same conclusion. He said, "Our belief at the beginning of a doubtful undertaking is the one thing—notice that carefully—the one thing that assures the successful outcome of our venture."

Long before William James, Jesus Christ said the same thing: "If thou canst believe, all things are possible to him that believeth" (Mark 9:23). It is amazing what belief can accomplish.

One day Andrew brought his brother Simon to Christ. Carefully the Lord sized him up. He saw in him certain weaknesses, but He also saw possibilities. So Christ said to him, "Thou art Simon the son of Jona: thou shalt be called Cephas, which is by interpretation, A stone" (John 1:42). He was saying, "You are one thing now, but I see in you possibilities of being something else. I believe in you." We know that at times the Lord's faith in Peter was severely tried, yet He kept on believing in him and eventually Peter became the man Jesus believed he could be.

Bishop Hazen Werner tells of being in the home of a woman whose husband had just died. She told of her husband's long nights of suffering and how she had cared for him, not having the money to employ a nurse. He wondered how she could have kept going, and she told him that the neighbors had kept their lights burning through the last few nights. She said, "I knew that they were thinking of us, feeling for us. I can't tell you how, but I got strength from it. It kept me up."

The fact that somebody is interested, that somebody cares, that somebody believes in us is often our strongest support.

EVERY PERSON NEEDS TO BE BELIEVED IN

A mother told me about her son, who had completely missed the way. Again and again he had broken her heart. What could she do? I told her that though she could do nothing else, she could keep on believing in him, that the most powerful force in any person's life is the faith that someone has in him. When we lose that, we lose everything.

There is a story told about Rupert Brooke, the great poet. He was about to sail from Liverpool. After he had gotten on board, he became aware that just about everyone there had someone on the dock waving good-bye. He felt a sudden loneliness. Then he spied a little boy—just a street urchin—down on the dock. He went back down the gang-plank and found that boy.

"Do you want to earn sixpence?" he asked. "Sure," said the boy. "Well," Brooke is reported to have said, "here it is. When the ship leaves, stand here and wave to me."

As the great ship moved away, the little boy stood there waving a dirty handkerchief. The heart of the poet was warmed and he was helped.

For several years now it has been my privilege to speak to large crowds in many places over the country. Occasionally someone asks me why I don't spend all my time in that way. But above all things else, I want to be pastor of a church. I want to have my own congregation; I want to belong to some people and feel that they belong to me. It means everything to have a congregation of people who claim me as their pastor. They know my faults and weaknesses, yet they pray for me and believe in me. That is worth more than anyone can measure. One of the saddest lines in the Bible is the word of the Psalmist, "No man cared for my soul" (142:4).

In Robert Sherwood's play, *Abe Lincoln in Illinois*, Abe speaks of Ann Rutledge: "And then—when I saw her, I knew there could be beauty and purity in people, like the purity you sometimes see in the sky at night. When I took hold of her hand, and held it, all fear, all doubt, went out of me. I believed in God. I'd have been glad to work for her until I die, to get for her everything out of life that she wanted. If she thought I could do it, then I could."

We hear a lot said about gossip in the church and criticism of one another, but actually, there isn't much of that. The very basis of the Christian fellowship is that people love and trust each other. And the better we know Christ, the more we believe. Someone has said, "In the company of sinners, He dreamed of saints." To one who had missed the way, He said, "Neither do I condemn thee: go, and sin no more" (John 8:11). He did not minimize her sin, but neither did He minimize her possibilities. Even though He saw her shameful past, He saw her future could be different.

We need somebody to believe in us. We need to learn to believe in other people. But more important, we need to realize the belief Christ has in us and what it means.

Study carefully the life of Christ, and you will see that never one time did He speak harshly to a sinner. Instead, He saw in a fallen one new possibilities and He invited that one into the new way. But sometimes it is awfully hard to accept His belief in us, because it is a very demanding thing.

A certain young man came to Him seeking the life that only Christ could give. The story says Jesus loved him, but though He loved with a love that would never let him go, He also loved with a love that would never let him off. He might have said, "Well, I don't expect you to be perfect. I will excuse your sins," but He didn't say that. He said, "If you want to follow me, you must change your life; you must rid yourself of that wrong." The young man turned from Christ and went away (Mark 10:17-22).

We feel His eyes upon us. We realize the possibilities He sees in us. We know He believes we can be something better than what we are. Yet sometimes we don't want to pay the price He demands. We disobey His commands, we fail to live up to His ideals for us, we are ashamed of things we have done yet we are unwilling to change. He reaches out and places a firm hand on our shoulders, but we twist away from that hand. Sometimes we defiantly say, "It's my life; I will live it as I please."

But across nearly two thousand years, Christ has been reaching out to men and expressing His belief in men, and the fact of His belief has been the magic that has changed more lives than anything else this world has ever known. Though Simon Peter failed Him again and again, Christ never let him go. After His resurrection, He still kept believing in Peter. One morning at breakfast He turned to Peter and said, "Simon, son of Jonas, lovest thou me more than these? . . . Feed my lambs" (John 21:15). Not a word of his past failures did Christ speak. Instead, He gave him a purpose, something to live for.

A tornado swept through a town in which a paralyzed mother lay confined to her bed. When the tornado struck she was at home alone with her two small children. The need of her children, however, was stronger than the paralysis in her legs. Slowly she got up; painfully she walked into the next room and, taking her children by the hand, walked with them out of the house. Being a mother in a time of danger gave her a sense of mission that was strong enough to overcome her limitations

And so, Christ comes into our lives—lives that are crippled and handicapped in so many ways. He gives us a purpose in life and He believes we can fulfill that purpose, and His belief becomes a magic force that makes weak men strong, failing men triumphant, and bad men good.

ELIMINATE THE WORD IMPOSSIBLE

Take another glance at Peter. He was a man of strange contrasts when Christ first met him. Sometimes he showed great courage.

For example, that night in the garden of Gethsemane Peter drew his sword and stood up against an entire company of soldiers. Yet later the same night, when a girl asked him if he were a friend of Christ, he cursed and denied it vigorously. He had great ideas and wanted to do big things, but really in his heart he was a coward. But Christ kept believing in him, and gradually Peter became a changed man.

Later on, Peter was arrested for preaching Christ and was put in prison. The next day in court Peter spoke courageously in his defense. There was no quivering, no fear, no hesitation about him. He had become as solid as a rock, even as Christ said he would. And then we read this thrilling sentence: "Now when they saw the boldness of Peter and John, and perceived that they were unlearned and ignorant men, they marvelled; and they took knowledge of them, that they had been with Jesus" (Acts 4:13).

One of the greatest mistakes we make is to think that if we could just solve some particular problem, or change the outward circumstances of our lives, we would be happy. That is not true. The place to change is inside ourselves.

Let me suggest a simple exercise for one week. On the first day, keep a record with pencil and paper of how many times you say or even think the word, "impossible," or have kindred thoughts such as, "It is hopeless," "I can't do it," "It's too big for me," etc. Just before you go to bed check up on the number. The next day, keep a record again and concentrate on reducing the number of times you think a defeating thought. And so on through the week. It is marvelous what you can do for yourself. But because we are weak, let's take Christ into this with us; remember His words, "If thou canst believe, all things are possible to him that believeth" (Mark 9:23).

As a man yields his life to Christ, gradually Christ takes possession of him. St. Paul said, "Let this mind be in you, which was also in Christ Jesus" (Philippians 2:5). As He takes possession of our minds, we think as He thought. We eliminate the word, "impossible," from our vocabularies. We begin to believe and to act on our beliefs. Then a marvelous force begins to express itself in our lives; it is the magic of belief.

17.

LOOK AT SOMETHING BIG

HERE IS ONE of the grandest verses in the Bible: "When I consider thy heavens, the work of thy fingers, the moon and the stars, which thou hast ordained . . ." (Psalm 8:3).

Have you ever wondered why God made the world so beautiful, so impressive, so big? Nobody knows how big the heavens are with their millions, maybe billions, of stars. God didn't have to make it that big in order for the earth to exist. Why did God make it so that every morning the

86

glory of a sunrise would come over the earth and every evening the quiet beauty of a sunset? He could have arranged it so the day would come and go in some less impressive manner.

Have you ever looked at a great mountain range and wondered why God made those high peaks? God could have left the mountains out of His creation. Mountains aren't really good for anything. They can't be cultivated; and beyond a certain point, they don't even grow trees. We do not need mountains in order to live on this earth.

I have flown across the trackless deserts of the West. As I looked at the endless miles of hot sand, I wondered why God made them that way. The deserts aren't good for anything. No food can grow there; the few creatures who live there are worthless to mankind.

Most impressed am I when I look at the ocean. Nobody really knows how big the ocean is. In places it is literally miles deep. It seems an awful waste. God could have fixed His creation so that rain could come without creating that vast reservoir of water. Why did He make the ocean?

God had a reason for making oceans, mountains, skies, and deserts. He never wastes anything. The Psalmist said, "When I consider thy heavens. . . ." The tragedy is that many people live amid God's creation and never consider it. A thoughtless person once said to Helen Keller, "Isn't is awful to be blind?" She replied, "Not half so bad as to have two good eyes and never see anything."

I like the reply of the boy who, when someone rebuked him for saying "I seen," replied, "It is better to say 'I seen' and see something, than 'I saw' and never see anything."

We have a little dog at our house. His entire world is our backyard. He has never even noticed the sky. The only time he ever looks up into a tree is if he is trying to catch a squirrel that has climbed out of his reach. He knows us and likes to be with us, but if anyone else comes into his yard, he barks at them and resents their presence. God's wonderful creation is wasted as far as our little dog is concerned.

And there are people who are content with a mighty small world. They never "consider the heavens." They never really see anything big.

When I think of the marvelous creation of the Lord—the skies and seas, mountains and deserts—and wonder why God made it all, two answers come to my mind.

OUR GOD IS A GREAT GOD

The Psalmist says, "The heavens declare the glory of God" (19:1). The last time I was in New York I stood on top of the Empire State Building. I realized that whoever planned and built a building that big and high had big ideas, great abilities and resources. Little people could not have built it; they would not even have thought of it.

When you look into the face of the sky and consider something of its infinite size, you realize that no little God created it. He had to have big ideas and unlimited abilities. Truly we come to realize, "Our God is a great God." Realizing His greatness, we are not as afraid of what might happen in His world. Hitlers come and go, but they cannot defeat God. Our troubles seem hard to bear, but nothing can defeat the will and purposes of the Eternal Father.

I have watched colossal storms roar across the mountains. Heavy clouds come thundering in and everything gets dark. You begin to wonder if the world isn't going to be destroyed. Then, the clouds break up and you see the green mountainside bathed in sunlight. And you know that if you wait out the storm, there will be sunlight again. When we have trouble and everything seems lost, with a picture of the greatness of God in mind, we gain courage and calmness.

On the other hand, when the sun is shining and the breezes are gentle, we know it will not always remain so. Sooner or later it will cloud up and rain again. So we make preparation during the good weather for the bad that is sure to follow. Likewise, when we are blessed with a life that is smooth and good, we remember that we must be ready for the trouble that is sure to come.

Realizing the greatness of God, our minds are stretched to take the long view of life, not living for just the moment but considering the whole. It has been determined by Greyselinck, the geologist, that if a movie of the entire history of the earth were made, and if the film ran for twenty-four hours, the first half of it would show history that man knows nothing about. In the twenty-four hour film, the life of man on earth would consume only the last five seconds of the film.

Such truth leads one to think in terms of eternity. A father whose son was recently killed said to me, "I could not bear it, if I thought this was the end of my boy. But God has planned far beyond this life and one accident will not wreck Hs plans."

Such truth keeps one from surrendering to troubles, because all troubles are momentary. It makes us realize that, come sunshine or storm, life goes on toward the accomplishment of God's purposes. Nothing can defeat Him. He is greater than all His creation.

To Think Big Thoughts

"When I consider thy heavens . . ." said the Psalmist. The Bible ties man in with the bigness of nature. God endowed man with the capacity to "consider" His wonderful creation. He did it for a reason. When you meditate on the bigness of skies and seas, mountains and plains, it causes you to think big thoughts. And when you begin to think big, you begin to act big.

I was preaching in another state recently. One night after a service, the pastor began to tell me of one of their ministers who had gone wrong. He mentioned the man's name and suddenly I was cold all over.

One night soon after I had begun my own ministry, I went to preach in a little country church. I got there early and was sitting on the steps waiting for the people to come. The first one to arrive was a young man. He sat down beside me and we sat there looking at the stars and talking about how they came to be. Then I called him by name and said, "God made you, too," and we talked about his life.

At the close of my sermon that night, that young man came forward, put his hand in my hand and his life in God's hand. He felt the call to the ministry. He responded to Him who said, "Go ye into all the world and preach the gospel." He worked hard and made a good beginning, but somewhere along the way, he began to look down and lost his vision. I don't know where he is now, but I am making every effort to find him. I believe I can persuade him to look with me again into the heavens. I believe I can bring new hope to his little broken-hearted wife. And I believe God will give him another chance and that he can still make good.

It has been said:

> Two men look out through the same bars:
> One sees mud, and the other sees stars.

God put the stars there hoping we will look up and look big at life. When you see big things—like heavens, mountains, and oceans—you think big thoughts. And when you think big thoughts, your life begins to grow and you rise above a multitude of little things that would hurt you.

When Glenn Clark was a little boy, he had a nurse who foolishly tried to frighten him into being good. She told him that if little boys acted badly and didn't say their prayers, they would go blind and would not be able to see. After he went to bed and the light was turned off, he would begin to wonder if he could still see. So he would slip out of bed, go over to the window to see if he could see the stars.

"When I consider thy heavens. . . ." Some people become blind to the great things of God. Wrong living has a way of obscuring our vision. Neglect can also destroy our power to "consider the heavens." Maybe right now it would be well for you to stand before the window of prayer, and look again into the face of the Father.

18.

JESUS' FORMULA
FOR PEACE OF MIND

ONCE A YOUNG MAN made a list of the things he would like to possess in life. He listed health, love, beauty, talent, power, riches, and fame. He showed his list to a wise man much older in years. After reading the list, the older and wiser man replied: "An excellent list, well digested in content and set down in not-unreasonable order. But it appears, my young friend, that you have omitted the most important element of all. You have forgotten the one ingredient, lacking which, each possession becomes a hideous torment, and your list, as a whole, an intolerable burden."

"And what is that missing ingredient?" the young man asked.

With a pencil the old man crossed out the young man's entire list. Then, underneath he wrote down just three words—peace of mind. The young man was Joshua Liebman who later wrote the book, *Peace of Mind*, which has sold more than a million copies. In fact, there have been many books written on that subject and all of them have had large sales. Because more than any other thing—even health, power or riches—we want peace of mind.

But you do not need to read a book to find the pathway to peace of mind. Jesus summed the entire matter up in just eleven verses, Matthew 6:24-34. Notice the basic principle He sets forth: "No man can serve two masters: for either he will hate the one, and love the other; or else he will hold to the one, and despise the other. Ye cannot serve God and mammon."

The principle is clear: a divided mind is fighting against itself and thus it cannot be at peace. Your inner war must be ended by your complete, wholehearted decision. While life demands many decisions, Jesus would have us realize that basically there is just one decision. Settle that one and you settle them all. The decision is: God or mammon. The word mammon represents the desires of our body, and God represents the longings of our soul. Make up your mind which is most important and give yourself wholly to it. Then you will have peace of mind.

On one occasion Jesus said, "Remember Lot's wife" (Luke 17:32). He might have reminded us of her in connection with this most basic of all decisions, because she is a perfect example of indecision. As a member of a family that gave us our greatest prophets and purest saints, she had within her the faith of her family. She knew God, and from her childhood she had known the meaning of prayer.

But along with her husband she moved into Sodom, the city of mammon. More important, Sodom moved into her. She wanted God, but she also wanted Sodom. Finally the day of final choice came. She made a start toward God, but she looked back toward Sodom. Reaching for the stars with one hand and fingering the mud with the other, she revealed her divided heart, and she ended with misery and eventual destruction.

We must make the choice—"Ye cannot serve God and mammon."

What is the most complete picture of restlessness to be seen? I think it is the sea. Again and again I have stood upon the seashore and watched the constant movements of the sea. I have never seen it still, even for one moment.

Ceaselessly the ocean tosses itself upon the shores and then runs back again. Why can't the sea lie down and be still? Because it is the victim of a divided mind. The voices of the sky are calling to it. The ocean is drawn upon by the magnets in the heavens. But the muddy old world holds on and demands, "Stay with me." The ocean can never completely decide, and neither can it stop its ears to the voices it hears from the earth and from the heavens. Thus it is always tossing; it never finds rest and peace.

So it is with me and with you. Jesus said, "No man can serve two masters." Until you choose your master, you will never have peace of mind. There are two forces within every person struggling to become the master. One is his ideals, the call of the high life, the desire to be good and godly. The other is his selfish desires, his worldly nature. Goethe said it is regrettable that nature made only one man of him when there is material aplenty for both a rogue and a gentleman. We may choose the low life, but even then we will not have peace because God will never leave us alone. It is as Augustine said, "Man is restless until he finds his rest in Thee, O God."

COMMITMENT

Consider the picture of our Lord when ". . . he stedfastly set his face to go to Jerusalem . . ." (Luke 9:51). He heard the voice of inclination; He heard the voice of God. There was no wavering. ". . . he stedfastly set his face." Three elements made up His decision. First, there was commitment. There was no longer any question. The issue was settled. We need to deal honestly, even ruthlessly, with ourselves at this point. It is so easy to drift along without fully making up our minds. And most of our troubles grow out of indecision.

Have you read the book, *Quo Vadis?* The title means, "Whither goest thou?" Peter had failed to convert the Romans and he determined to leave the city. On his way out, Christ appeared to him and said, *"Quo vadis?"* The question made Peter realize he was turning away from the work he had been called to do. So he turned around and went back, even though it eventually meant a martyr's death. But the main point is, Peter found the peace going back that he lost running away.

COURAGE

Out of commitment comes the second element, courage. Had you looked into the Lord's face as He turned toward Jerusalem, you would have seen no fear. It has been pointed out that we do not run because we are afraid; rather we are afraid because we run. Face up to it squarely and honestly; refuse to run. An old ship captain shouted to his sailors during a heavy storm, "Keep her facing it, always facing it, that's the way to get through." With decision comes courage.

". . . he stedfastly set his face to go to Jerusalem." He made the commitment and then as a result came courage. The two go hand in hand. We are afraid only until we fully decide.

CALMNESS

As a result of commitment and courage, something else comes—calmness. Even as Christ hung upon the pain-drenched cross, He spoke a calm valedictory: Father, into Thy hands I commend my spirit" (Luke 23:46). I know of no other way to attain calm peace in our own minds and hearts.

Very often I get in an airplane to go somewhere. I always go through the same mental routine. When I sit down and fasten the seatbelt, I begin to wonder if this plane will fly. The engines start and I listen to see if they are running smoothly. Slowly the plane begins to move down the runway. The pilot can stop and go back until he reaches a certain point. That point is where the speed is so great that he couldn't stop; he must go on. It is the point of commitment. Then I settle down because there is no turning back. I must put my faith in the plane. And because I believe in the plane, I am not afraid and I feel calm as we fly into the sky.

Several years ago Joshua Liebman wrote *Peace of Mind*. Later Fulton J. Sheen wrote *Peace of Soul*. Since one of those was a Jew and the other a Catholic, the publisher suggested to Ralph W. Sockman, a Protestant, that he write on the same theme. He did write the book—entitled, *How to Believe*. I think he showed keen insight, because when one learns to believe he finds peace of mind and soul.

Because I believe in the airplane, I am willing to commit my life to the principle that it is able to carry me safely on my journey. Likewise, when I believe in God, I commit my life into His hands, believing that He can and will carry me through. And believing in God, being committed to God, I find courage and calmness. So Jesus said, "No man can serve two masters." Make your commitment.

Then read what Christ says following that verse: "Therefore I say unto you, Take no thought [be not anxious] for your life . . ." (Matthew 6:25). He points out that we do not need to worry about clothes, food, and the material things of life. Look at the birds of the air and the lilies of the field. God abundantly provides for them; shall He not do much more for one of His own children?

Jesus concludes by saying, "But seek ye first the kingdom of God, and his righteousness . . ." (6:33) Put God first. Decide once and for all on the right. Now notice—Christ doesn't say we will be denied the things we want in life. He says, ". . . all these things shall be added unto you" (6:33). The picture we have that the godly life must be one of hard sacrifice is wrong. The Psalmist said, "[I have] not seen the righteous forsaken . . ." (37:25). Come to think of it, I never have either. Have you?

19.

THE PEACE HE GIVES

ONE OF THE MOST appealing verses in the Bible is this one: "Peace I leave with you, my peace I give unto you: not as the world giveth, give I unto you. Let not your heart be troubled, neither let it be afraid" (John 14:27).

It makes us feel fine just to read that verse. Right now read it again. We feel drawn to those words as a thirsty man is drawn to a cool spring. More than anything else in this life we want inner peace. We are tired of living with our inner conflicts, tension, and turmoil; and we would rather possess peace of mind and heart than anything else.

Peace is not something we search for and work for. Jesus

said, "my peace I give unto you." He gives it freely. All that remains is for us to accept it. But in order to be able to accept His peace, there are three other things we must accept from Him—His pardon, His Presence, and His purposes. Let's look at each of those.

HIS PARDON

First, we must accept His pardon. We have in mind some sin we have committed, some wrong of which we are ashamed. A sense of guilt haunts us, and we are never able to get away from it. We are sorry for what we have done, we refuse to do it again, and sincerely we ask God to forgive us. God always forgives those who ask Him to and who really mean it. We remember the Bible says, "If we confess our sins, he is faithful and just to forgive us our sins, and to cleanse us from all unrighteousness" (I John 1:9).

But there is a curious quirk within the human mind that makes it hard for us to accept God's forgiveness. Knowing we have done wrong, we feel we deserve punishment, and we live in constant dread and fear that something bad is going to happen to us. Subconsciously we say, "I've done wrong and someday I will pay for it." I went to the dentist the other day. He didn't hurt me, but I kept expecting him to any moment. Thus I could never relax as long as I was in his chair. And the constant dread and fear of some dire punishment for our sins robs life of all chance of deep inner peace.

Well, one way to gain faith in the forgiveness of God is to practice forgiving other people. In fact, this is essential because Jesus said, "For if you forgive men their trespasses, your heavenly Father will also forgive you . . ." (Matthew 6:14).

In his book, *Learning to Have Faith,* Dr. John A. Redhead imagines a man with two buckets, one filled with water and the other with oil. Both are full to the brim. You cannot pour the oil from one bucket into the other because both are full. Also, the two would not mix.

Now, imagine that one of those buckets is you and the

other is God. He wants to pour His forgiving love into your life, but you are holding resentment toward some person and thus you have no room for God. Also, God's loving mercy and your unforgiving spirit won't mix. So before you can accept His forgiveness, you must forgive that other person.

"My peace I give unto you," said Christ. Before you can accept His peace, you must first accept His pardon.

Some have come to me in a hopeless condition, feeling they have committed some unpardonable sin. I explain that the only unpardonable sin is to become so hardened by sin that the soul loses its feeling. The very fact that one feels a sense of guilt is positive proof of his ability to receive pardon. So I suggest to such a person that instead of concentrating on his sins, he fill his mind with God's promises to forgive his sins. Note these words:

". . . Him that cometh to me I will in no wise cast out" (John 6:37); ". . . whosoever believeth in him should not perish, but have everlasting life" (John 3:16); "As far as the east is from the west, so far hath he removed our transgressions from us" (Psalm 103:12); "And Jesus said unto her, Neither do I condemn thee: go, and sin no more" (John 8:11).

Fix those words in your mind—"Him that cometh" . . . "Whosoever" . . . "removed our transgressions from us" . . . "sin no more." Those are God's words to you—accept His forgiveness and believe that you have received it.

HIS PRESENCE

Second, to accept His peace, we must accept His Presence. At the beginning of World War II in England, the authorities evacuated the children from the areas under bombardment. But they soon discovered their mistake. The children became emotionally upset. Though they were safe, and all their physical necessities were provided for, being deprived of the love and companionship of their parents did them great harm.

So it is with us. We may live in the finest house, eat the best food, and have all the things money can buy. Still,

97

without the fellowship of our heavenly Father, we remain restless and without inner peace.

The Bible says, "Be still, and know that I am God" (Psalm 46:10). Also ". . . in quietness and in confidence shall be your strength . . ." (Isaiah 30:15). Stillness—quietness: that is the greatest need of multitudes in the noisy, hurrying life of today. Note an amazing statement of Starr Daily, a man who knows much about the art of spiritual healing. He said, "No man or woman of my acquaintance who knows how to practice silence and does it has ever been sick to my knowledge."

Surely the practice of silence is more soothing and healing than most medicines. How can one learn the art of stillness, of quietness, of silence? Pascal, the great scientist, said: "After observing human kind over a long period of years, I came to the conclusion that one of man's great troubles is his inability to be still."

I was on a plane once when the pilot announced over the speaker, "I am now going to cut the motors momentarily to make an adjustment to allow us to climb higher." To climb higher, man needs to learn to "cut his motor" and to make adjustments.

The Bible says, "Be still, and know that I am God." There is tremendous power to be gained from completely silencing the mind, but it isn't easy to do. Here is one way to accomplish it:

Go alone to the quietest place available to you. Do not read. Do not write. Begin by letting a mental picture of the most peaceful scene you have ever witnessed pass across your mind. Some months ago, I spent two weeks at Sea Island. Under the spell of that lovely place, every bit of the tension and hurry of life was drained out of me and I became completely relaxed. But for me, the benefits of Sea Island are not limited to the actual days I was there. I enjoy that experience again and again as I sit quietly and begin to see in my mind the ocean, the waves rolling up on the beach and back again, the gentle swaying of the sea grass. Through the power of imagination, one can quickly transport himself back into a peaceful scene and experience its healing influence.

Then, under that spell, begin to repeat audibly some

peaceful words. Words have great suggestive power. Speak words like earthquake, murder, house on fire, cancer, blood —and you feel nervousness. But words like tranquility, serenity, imperturbable—such words create within you the mood they describe. Repeat them aloud, slowly and thoughtfully.

Have you ever dropped a pebble into a very still pond and watched the tiny waves go out over the surface of the water? Now while your mind is quiet, drop into it some of the great truths of God from the Bible, such as: "The Lord is my shepherd; I shall not want" (Psalm 23:1); "Let not your heart be troubled: ye believe in God, believe also in me" (John 14:1); "The eternal God is thy refuge, and underneath are the everlasting arms . . ." (Deuteronomy 33:27).

Usually in this moment some lines of some of the songs I love will come to mind:

> What a friend we have in Jesus,
> All our sins and griefs to bear. . . .
>
> Jesus calls us, o'er the tumult
> Of our life's wild, restless sea,
> Day by day his sweet voice soundeth,
> Saying, "Christian follow me."

His Purposes

Then, realizing God's pardon and experiencing His Presence, you take the third step necessary to the acceptance of His peace: You accept God's purposes. One of the primary causes of inner tension is mental disorganization. We have not learned to take up one thing at a time and concentrate on that. And above the daily routine of life, we have no guiding goals and purposes.

We remember the experience of the Master in Gethsemane. He got away from the crowd, even away from his closest friends. He got quiet and alone with God and then He said, ". . . nevertheless not my will, but thine, be done"

99

(Luke 22:42). And who doubts but that in that moment all the inner strain and tension left Him. It is truly written, "In His will is our peace."

20.

WHAT CAN I BELIEVE ABOUT LUCK

Is THERE SUCH a thing as luck? Of course there is. Read Jesus' story of the Good Samaritan. A man was left wounded and half dead on the side of the road. Then Jesus said, "And by chance there came down a certain priest that way" (Luke 10:31).

"By chance"—a lot of things in your life happen by chance. You did not plan it; no one planned it—it just happened. It was pure and simple luck. Luck may be good or it may be bad—it is something that happens that was not planned or designed and could not be foreseen. And one of the bewildering facts of life is that many of the important happenings in our lives seem to come by chance or luck.

When I was a student at Wofford College in Spartanburg, South Carolina, my entire life was changed just by chance. I had a job for the summer in New York. Then I was going to the School of Religion at Duke the following year. It was all fixed. Just about a month before school was out, a man in New Jersey, the father of one of our ministers in North Georgia, died.

Because of the sudden death of his father, it was necessary for this minister to give up his work and go back home to meet the emergency. This left a church without a pastor, and to fill the vacancy several moves had to be made. Finally they had one little church left. Someone happened to mention my name to the district superintendent. He wrote offering me the church. I took it. I didn't go to New York. That fall, I went to Emory. I have often wondered what my life would have been if a man in New Jersey had not died suddenly. Or if he had died a month earlier or a month later. It was just chance—but my entire life will always be different because of it.

How did you meet your wife or your husband? I was talking to a couple the other day who told me they met on a blind date. Neither of them planned it—it was just luck. You probably met the one you married by luck. (Remember, there is both good and bad luck.) Some people say you are destined to marry just one particular person, but the fact is you could have married one of many and been just as happy. I heard about a husband who was so devoted to his wife that when she died, he had printed on her tombstone, "The light of my life is gone out." But about six months later, he met another woman and happily married her. Whereupon someone wrote on his first wife's tombstone, "But he struck another match."

In his book, *Christ the Truth*, Archbishop William Temple tells about a man walking down the street. A sudden gust of wind blew over a chimney on a house; one of the bricks hit the man on the head and killed him. The wind had blown against that chimney many times, but this particular wind happened to blow it over and this man happened to be walking under it at that particular second. You cannot explain a thing like that except by saying it was pure chance or luck. If the man had been a second earlier or later he would not have been hit.

Many of life's most important happenings come by luck or chance. But that doesn't mean that life is determined by luck. Rather is your life determined by your reaction to your luck. Luck can either ruin us or make us—it depends not on our luck, but on us.

TWO THINGS TO KNOW

(1) Luck will ruin your life if you count on it instead of on careful preparation and hard work. One of the temptations of life is to go lazily along waiting for something good to happen—believing what is to be will be, no matter what we do about it. That attitude kills your soul and makes you

101

a careless, shiftless person. As you go through life, you may run into good luck but let this be remembered: You won't run into anything if you aren't running.

Matthew Arnold said it well:

> We do not what we ought;
> What we ought not, we do;
> And lean upon the thought
> That chance will bring us through.
>
> —*Empedocles on Etna*

(2) Luck will ruin your life if you use it as an alibi for your failures. We have a way of excusing ourselves by saying, "That's just my luck." When you say that, you become blind to your real self. You do not see your own failures, and thus you do not feel inspired to improve yourself. Blaming defeat on luck causes you to sit back and accept it.

When you go to a football game, you see some player take a hard fall. But he never just sits in the middle of the field bemoaning his bad luck, saying, "Why did this happen to me? What have I done to deserve this? Why did I have to be the one who got hit?" Instead, he gets up and gets back into the game.

On the other hand, the existence of luck or chance in life can bring out faith and courage within us. You never develop faith unless you are willing to take a chance, and if all life were a sure thing, you would have no need for faith. The fact that you are willing to dream and dare in spite of the element of chance develops your character.

The farmer plants his crop in the spring. He spends money on seed, fertilizer, and labor, yet he is taking a chance on the weather. He may lose everything if there is too much rain or too little rain. In one sense, he is a gambler; but in another sense, he is very different from the gambler at a card table or a dog race. The gambler at a card table is destroying his character by counting on luck, while the farmer develops his character by his efforts to overcome the elements of chance. One is trying to get something for nothing. The other is paying the price and daring to risk his efforts because of his faith.

When a mother loves her child, she is taking a chance.

102

That child may later break her heart, but the element of chance is what creates real love. This life cannot be lived on the basis of everything being certain and sure. Those who rise to life's heights are those whose faith and love grow bigger than anything that might happen.

But something else must be said about luck. The Bible says, "Be not deceived; God is not mocked: for whatsoever a man soweth, that shall he also reap" (Galatians 6:7). This is a law-abiding universe, and life will not ultimately be unjust. In the end, it all works out—not according to luck, but according to the laws and purposes of Almighty God.

While we know that much happens in life by luck or chance, we also know that this is a law-abiding universe and nothing happens that can defeat God and His purposes. We sometimes say, "Anything can happen," but that is a mistake.

Not everything can happen because God has kept His hand on this world and on our lives. As we see in the illustration of a child in its nursery, the parents do not cover the floor with a featherbed—thus, in learning to walk, the child may fall on the hard floor and hurt itself. This is part of the process of learning to walk. By putting the child in the nursery, the parents in a sense make it possible for the child to fall.

But on the other hand, the parents take certain precautions. They do not put razor blades or carbolic acid within reach of the child. Beyond a certain point, the child is protected. So has God dealt with His children on earth. Some things can happen, but God has so arranged it that nothing can happen that man cannot use for definite gain.

God has a plan and a purpose for every life. Something may break into that plan, but if I am faithful to God, nothing can defeat it. If I put a big rock in the bed of a tiny stream, I stop its flow for a time, but soon the water finds a way around the obstruction and makes its way to the big river. So with life. There is always a way around our obstructions, and we can keep going until we get into the mighty river of God's eternal purpose.

Once I was in Talladega, Alabama, for a revival. While there, I visited the school for the deaf and the blind—the largest in the world. I sat in the classroom and watched the teachers patiently working with six- and seven-year-old children who were totally deaf. Never have I been so thrilled as I was when I saw how they were teaching those children to overcome their handicaps.

The school for the blind in Talladega has a band. One of the finest men there is the leader of that band. He, too, is blind. He leads by blowing a horn. When he was six years old, his eyes became infected. The physician gave a prescription; the parents had it filled and put it in the little boy's eyes. But there was a mistake—either the doctor made it, or the druggist, or the parents. Anyway, by chance or luck, he became blind. In spite of his blindness, he has become a wonderful man. And after all, wasn't that God's purpose for him? Who knows but that in overcoming his bad luck, he is now a better man.

When Judas died, a vacancy was left among the twelve disciples. Instead of waiting to find the best man, they cast lots. Matthias was selected. That place should have gone to St. Paul. It was mere luck that Paul missed it. But instead of being bitter, he went right ahead. No one ever heard of Matthias again, but Paul rose to a place of eminence. He didn't let a piece of bad luck spoil his life.

One thing more. In considering the things that happen by luck or chance, we must take the long view of life. After all, it doesn't matter whether I live in Atlanta or Houston, whether I am a preacher or a carpenter, whether I make a lot of money or a little. Read again the story of Dives and Lazarus (Luke 16:19-31). Dives seemed to have all the good luck and Lazarus the bad—but maybe it was the other way around. Dives' good luck blinded him to the really important things in life, and in the end he suffered for it.

In moments of good luck or bad luck, the main thing is to learn the purposes of God and not let our luck keep us from those purposes. It isn't your luck that really matters—it is what you do about it.

21.

WHEN OPPORTUNITY KNOCKS FOR THE LAST TIME

HOW MANY FRIENDS do you have? That is, how many do you have who will stand by you to the utmost and to the end? Who will keep on loving you and never let you down, no matter what happens? We sing, "What a friend we have in Jesus."

Other than that One who seeks to be the friend of every man, St. Paul had two such friends. One was Luke, "the beloved physician." Luke stuck with him when the last one had forsaken him. The other was Timothy, whom he called, "my own son in the faith" (I Timothy 1:2). It is believed by many that when Paul had been stoned by the mob at Lystra, dragged out of the city's gates and left for dead, it was Timothy who went out and found him after the mob had left, put his arms about his bleeding body, carried him to safety, and nursed him back to health.

Finally the great Apostle had about reached the end. He was in jail in Rome. Probably he would be executed. But even if he should be spared, his frail and tired body would not last much longer. He writes two letters to his friend, Timothy. They are kind and gentle and loving letters. Above all he longs to see him. He writes: "Do thy diligence to come shortly unto me" (II Timothy 4:9).

It is cold in that dreary jail. He remembers an old coat he had left in Troas. He asks Timothy to pick it up on the way and bring it. The hours go by slowly in jail, so he tells Timothy to bring him some books he had left, too. He comes to the end of the letter and he adds these words, ". . . come before winter."

Why "before winter"? Because when winter came navigation closed in the Mediterranean. If Timothy didn't come before winter, it would be too late. It was before winter or never. I wonder what Timothy did? I want to believe that he dropped everything and went. But on the other hand, he was busy. There was a church to be built in Ephesus, some elders to be ordained in Colossae, a series of services scheduled for Miletus.

He might have said, "I'll clear up these pressing matters first. Then, as soon as spring comes and the boats start running again, I'll go and spend a long time with my dear friend." If he took that course, when he landed in Rome, he rushed to the jail. But when he asked for Paul, the jailor said, "Why, they cut his head off three months ago. Every time the key turned in his jail door, he asked, 'Has Timothy come?' As we led him out that morning he looked down the road, but his friend never showed up."

On the other hand, I want to believe Timothy came "before winter" and walked by his friend's side down the jail's corridor that last morning. For all of us there come opportunities that must be taken "before winter." Put them off and it is too late.

There is an old saying, "Opportunity knocks but once." That is not true. Opportunity knocks many times. But it is true that opportunity has a way of knocking for its last time. "Come before winter," said St. Paul to Timothy. It was "before winter" or never.

Back in the year 1915, Dr. Clarence E. Macartney preached on the subject, "Come Before Winter". He repeated that sermon every year for forty years. Many wonderful results came from it. One night in Philadelphia, a medical student heard that sermon. The words, "Come before winter," kept ringing in his ears. He needed to study but first he wrote that letter to his mother he had been neglecting. He went out and mailed it.

The very next day, a telegram came telling him to hurry home. His mother was dying. It was a long trip and he finally got there. Under her pillow he found the letter he had written. It had meant so much to her. When he got back to Philadelphia, he thanked Dr. Macartney for preaching on "Come Before Winter."

Paul wasn't content merely to ask Timothy to come as

106

soon as he could. He added "before winter." Timothy might forget there would come the time when it would be impossible to come. You know, we need that reminder—"before winter." I conduct many funerals and I find it easier to speak words of comfort when loving friends have sent flowers. But sometimes I look at those flowers and wish they had come "before winter."

Dr. Macartney tells of a man who was under the bondage of liquor. One night he was in his hotel room; his craving came upon him; he reached for the phone for a bell boy. Suddenly he seemed to hear a voice. It was saying, "This is your hour. Yield now and it will destroy you. Conquer it now, and you are its master forever." Such moments come to every person. There are decision times and, once passed by, they are gone forever.

"Come before winter." Little boys and girls have a way of saying that. Every father plans on being a pal to his children. But young fathers need to get established in business; there is work to do. And golf, and dinner meetings, and the need to sleep past Sunday-school hour on Sunday, and this and that. Wouldn't it be wonderful if we could put our children in a deep freeze and keep them there until we had time for them? But children have a habit of growing up and getting away. If we love our children, it must be "before winter."

There is ill feeling between you and someone else. Maybe it is all his fault. Maybe it is yours. Maybe it is neither one's fault. Life is too short for that sort of thing. We mean to settle it, but we keep putting it off. Eventually it will have gone too far, or it will be too late. We need to settle it "before winter."

Whittier was right:

> For of all sad words of tongue or pen,
> The saddest are these: "It might have been!"
> —*Maud Muller*, Stanza 53

The winter comes—opportunity has knocked its last time.

Isabella Braham told about receiving a thousand pounds unexpectedly. Immediately she gave a tithe, one hundred pounds, and wrote in her diary a revealing note about human nature, "Quick, quick, before my heart gets hard." The Bible speaks of giving "upon the first day of the week." I know people who intended to give, but they held on until they lost their willingness. "Come before winter!"

I am one who believes the church is important. It is important for the sake of the community. It is even more important for the sake of the individual members. But the only kind of church membership that means anything is active membership. During the years I have been pastor of a church, I have asked hundreds of people, "What church do you belong to?" Proudly they answer Baptist, or Methodist, or Presbyterian, or some other church. I have never met one person who was ashamed of belonging to some church. But I then ask, "What church in this city do you belong to?" And often, much too often, the answer is, "I haven't moved my membership." The years are slipping by. So many times my phone has rung and a tearful voice has said, "Will you conduct his funeral? He never joined a church here." "Come before winter!"

We remember how our Lord walked along the shores of Galilee and said to certain men, "Come, follow me." There must have been an urgency in His appeal because we read they "left all, rose up, and followed Him" (Luke 5:28). They did not wait. The appeal of our Lord is, "Come before winter."

Winter is a time when it gets cold. Instead of growing, the leaves on the trees turn brown and die. Winter also comes to the human heart. There are many decisions we must make "before winter," if we are to ever make them at all. Has winter come to your heart, as far as your love for God and your interest in Christ is concerned? Ask yourself some questions:

Do you say your prayers at night before going to bed as you used to? Does the singing of an old hymn give the same thrill it once did? Can you miss the services in your church without caring? Can you speak profanity without being shocked at yourself? The prophet Jeremiah said, "The harvest is past, the summer is ended, and we are not saved" (Jeremiah 8:20).

"Come before winter," Paul urged Timothy. If he waited, navigation would close down, there would be no boats running, and his chance would be gone. Yes—opportunity knocks many times, but eventually it knocks for its last time.

22.

WHY AND HOW TO READ THE BIBLE

To BE PERFECTLY frank, most people do not enjoy reading the Bible. And the fact is, most people do not read the Bible very much. This is true of both those in the church and those outside the church. It would be painfully embarrassing to poll a modern church congregation to find out exactly how much time each person gives to Bible reading.

Of course, we honor and respect the Bible. If the government were to pass a law forbidding us to read it, we would revolt. If some person makes a disparaging remark about the blessed Book, we resent it furiously. We take pride in possessing a copy, and most homes have several copies. We buy it in expensive leather bindings, and we all agree the Bible is the most important of all books. But still we must admit we don't read it very much.

Countless thousands of people have made a resolution to read the Bible all the way through, and some do, but most have found their enthusiasm failing by the time they finish Genesis. If they get through Exodus, Leviticus usually about ends the matter and the Bible is put carefully aside. Compared with television programs, the picture magazines, the romantic novels, and all the other things we have to claim our attention, most people find the Bible a rather dull and uninteresting book. Many who do read it regularly put it in the class of taking medicine—something we don't like, but we force ourselves to do it anyway.

When we do read the Bible, we get confused because we are reading about strange people and strange customs.

They would go to war in the name of the Lord, they would sacrifice their babies on the altar, a man would work seven years to get his wife—today if a boy doesn't get engaged after his first few dates with a girl, he begins looking further. They did not have airplanes as we do; not even cars were invented back then—and it is hard to get excited about people who rode in ox carts. Well, why should we read the Bible?

The answer is found in the opening and closing words of the Book itself. It begins: "In the beginning God. . . ." Its final words are: "The grace of our Lord Jesus Christ be with you all. Amen." Through the sixty-six books of the Bible, there is one golden thread running that ties it all together just as thread holds together a string of beads. That thread is: there is a God, a God who takes an interest in the affairs of men, a God whose power is present in the life of man today.

The Bible contains God's revelation of Himself to man. I know people say they see God in the sunset, in flowers, in the lives of other people, in the study of history and in other ways, but without the revelation of God in the Bible, I doubt if we would see Him in any of those other ways. Without the Bible, man would be almost totally ignorant of God. If God matters, reading the Bible matters. So the important lesson to learn is how to read that Book so as to really get help from it.

Suppose you decide you would like to discover for yourself some of the treasures of the Bible. How should you begin? Would you start with Genesis and read all the way through Revelation? That would be the most unrewarding way you could read it. About all you would get out of that is just being able to say you had read the Bible through.

START WITH MARK

To really get help and find joy in your Bible reading, begin with Jesus. All that was written before Him was in preparation for His coming. All that was written after Him was to interpret His coming. There are four books in the Bible about Jesus, and by all means, the one to start with is

St. Mark. Not only is it the shortest, it is also the most precious book the world possesses.

Get a picture of Mark in your mind. He was a boy in his early teens during Jesus' ministry. We think the Last Supper took place in his house. He saw the men slipping in that night, one or two together. He knew something was happening and, being a normal boy, he wanted to know what it was. He was not admitted into the room, but you may be sure he found a place where he could see and hear it all.

No doubt Jesus had visited Mark's home many times. Mark had come to know Him well, and to know Him was to love Him. He saw Judas leave, and it must have broken his heart. Teen-agers are usually disappointed when some adult lowers their ideals. Mark followed Jesus and the disciples into the Garden of Gethsemane. He heard the Master pray; he saw the soldiers take Him; he stood on the outskirts of His trials; he saw Him crucified. Most teen-age boys would have seen all that happen if they had been in Mark's place. Many believe it was Mark who said to the women that first Easter: "He is not here: . . . he is risen . . ." (Matthew 28:6).

Probably Simon Peter was his hero. Of all the disciples, Peter was the one most likely to be chosen. Mark traveled with Peter, and in Rome he was probably impressed with the soldiers. Most boys get a thrill out of courageous action as typified by a soldier. He listened as Peter preached. As they traveled about, he would ask Peter about events in the life of Jesus. Being a young man, he was interested in action. Peter was also a man of action. So doubtless they talked more about what He did than what He said.

One day in Rome, Mark saw Peter put to death. Tradition has it that Peter made only one request, and that was that he be crucified with his head down. He did not feel himself worthy to be crucified in the same position as his Lord was crucified. Knowing Peter and his passion to preach Christ, it is likely that he made another request. "Mark," he may have whispered just before his death, "I won't be able to preach about Him anymore, but I have told you the facts. Before you forget, write the story of His life down and pass it around to the Christians to read."

After Peter was buried, Mark slipped away somewhere and wrote the story as he remembered it. By this time, Mark was about fifty years old, but he had not lost the enthusiasm of his youth or his love for the Lord. What he wrote makes mighty interesting reading.

Three Ways We Should Read

(1) *Read uncritically.* As long as I live I will never forget the first time I saw my wife. I might have said to her, "The earring on your left ear is crooked." I say, I might have said that, but I didn't. The truth is I did not notice whether she had on earrings or not. I don't remember whether she was wearing a red dress or a blue one. I didn't see all those details. I just saw her.

I'll never forget seeing the ocean for the first time. I just stood and looked at as much of it as my eyes could take in. I didn't stop to analyze the water to see if it had the proper mixture of hydrogen and oxygen, or to see how much salt it contained. I just looked at the ocean and my heart was lifted up by the very greatness of what I saw.

Turn to St. Mark's Gospel and look at Jesus like that. Don't worry about every little detail; don't stop on some verse that is hard to understand. Read those sixteen short chapters as you would read any other story. Don't argue about Him or try to reason with Him. Just take a good long look at Him through the eyes of Mark. Get the full picture in your mind first.

(2) *Read imaginatively.* Let your mind carry you back across the centuries and make you one of those who was actually present in the days of His life on earth. In the first chapter of Mark, you will meet John the Baptist—rough, fearless, truly great. Listen as his big voice booms out like the roar of a cannon: ". . . There cometh one mightier than I after me, the latchet of whose shoes I am not worthy to stoop down and unloose" (1:7). Does John sound as if he were talking about some pale-faced, anemic goody-goody who was weak and flabby? No. He was mightier than John. Let Mark draw the pictures for you, and one by one, let those pictures come into your view.

(3) *Read devotionally.* You are not seeking information when you read the Bible. You are seeking to meet a person. Recall that in John's Gospel, Jesus is quoted as saying, ". . . he that hath seen me hath seen the Father . . ." (14:9). Do you have questions about God? Someone has said, "I had a thousand questions until I met Him."

Suppose you were to sit down and write a description of the kind of God you wish we had. Describe His character and His activity just as you would like it to be. Then, as you read Mark's Gospel, you will find your own description expressed better than you did it yourself. Jesus was just what we want God to be. The best news ever given to man is that God is like Jesus. When the moment comes that you see God, it will be the most wonderful moment in your life. That is what we should get out of reading the Bible.

23.

GO DOWN DEATH

LET'S TALK ABOUT DEATH. Some protest. We do not want to hear the word "death" even mentioned. We prefer to go on pretending there is no such thing as death. We keep our age a secret and refuse to believe we are getting older. To maintain the illusion of eternal youth, we enlist the aid of health clubs, dressmakers, tailors, and beauty parlors. We buy creams and lotions, hair dyes and vitamin pills.

We recall that Job said, "If a man die, shall he live again?" (Job 14:14). We emphasize the "if" as though there were some doubt about whether or not a man dies. More properly we should say. "When a man dies." We try to disguise death with flowers covering the casket. We prepare a dead body to make it look lifelike. We dress the body in beautiful clothes and color pale cheeks—but the dead body is without any life. Dodge the fact as we will, death is real.

Some of us try to be nonchalant about death. We take the attitude of living today and not bothering about what lies beyond. Maybe nothing lies beyond, we say. Or if there is something else, we'll face it when it comes. That seems smart to some, to others it seems brave. Until—until someone I profoundly love has entered into that experience. Even if I am unconcerned about myself, I would hate to admit that I had grown so cold and indifferent as not to love any other person enough to care. My child, my wife, my mother, my friend: when death comes to one of them, is it smart or brave for me to be nonchalant—*laissez-faire* —about death?

After the death of his wife, Arthur John Gossip preached: "You people in the sunshine *may* believe the faith, but we in the shadow *must* believe it. We have nothing else." Yes, now you may have a choice, but sooner or later comes a time when there is nothing else you can do but believe.

(1) Some refuse to think of death; (2) some are nonchalant about it; (3) others live in constant dread and fear of death. They read everything they can find on the subject, talk with all who will listen, but they cannot get the question off their minds.

(4) The Christian is also concerned about death, but with still a different attitude. Listen to the Christian sing: "We are marching to Zion, the beautiful city of God"; "I am bound for the promised land"; "There's a land that is fairer than day"; "When we've been there ten thousand years." For the Christian, death is not a monster to be feared, it is a friend to be embraced.

The Christian believes in Him who said: "And whosoever liveth and believeth in me shall never die" (John 11:26); "In my Father's house are many mansions. . . . I go to prepare a place for you. . . . that where I am, there ye may be also. . . . because I live, ye shall live also" (John 14).

Do you believe this?

James Weldon Johnson wrote a wonderful poem, "Go Down Death." It came out of his childhood memories of

114

the sermons of the old Negro preachers. Death is an angel in heaven—God is speaking:

> And God said: Go down, Death, go down,
> Go down to Savannah, Georgia,
> Down in Yamacraw,
> And find Sister Caroline.
> She's borne the burden and heat of the day,
> She's labored long in my vineyard,
> And she's tired—
> She's weary.
> Go down, Death, and bring her to me

. . . .

> While we were watching round her bed,
> She turned her eyes and looked away,
> She saw what we couldn't see:
> She saw Old Death. She saw Old Death
> Coming like a falling star.
> But Death didn't frighten Sister Caroline;
> He looked to her like a welcome friend.
> And she whispered to us: I'm going home,
> And she smiled and closed her eyes.

. . . .

> Weep not, weep not,
> She is not dead;
> She's resting in the bosom of Jesus.

Peter Marshall, in his sermon entitled "Go Down Death," tells a wonderful story of a little boy with an incurable illness. Month after month the mother tenderly nursed him. But as the time went by, the little fellow gradually began to understand he would not live. One day he quietly said, "Mother, what is it like to die? Mother, does it hurt?"

Tears filled the mother's eyes and she fled to the kitchen to see about something on the stove. She knew the question must be faced. She leaned against the kitchen cabinet, her knuckles pressed white against the wall, and breathed a hurried prayer, "Lord, tell me how to answer him." And the Lord did tell her; immediately she knew what to say.

115

She returned to his room. "Kenneth," she said, "you remember when you were a tiny boy you used to play so hard, when night came you would be too tired even to undress, and you would tumble into mother's bed and fall asleep? That was not your bed—it was not where you belonged.

"In the morning you would wake up and find yourself in your own bed in your own room. Your father had come—with big strong arms—and carried you away. Kenneth, death is just like that. We just wake up some morning and find ourselves in the other room—our own room where we belong—because the Lord Jesus loved us."

The little lad never questioned again. Several weeks later he fell asleep just as she had said. That is what death is like.

And there is something else to be said. The pain and weakness caused by his illness was gone—forever. Some other things will be gone with death: endless processions of fears that have tortured someone's mind day and night; the drunkard's thirst, like the fires of hell; the bitter disappointments and the crushing pain of defeat; the tears of sorrow that shut out the sunlight; the deformed body; the broken dreams; broken hearts; and so many more things.

It is as John said, "And God shall wipe away all tears from their eyes; and there shall be no more death, neither sorrow, nor crying, neither shall there be any more pain: for the former things are passed away" (Revelation 21:4).

THE SIMPLE STORY

What is it that takes the fear of death out of the mind of the Christian? It is Easter. Do not fail to hear the news as it is proclaimed. The same story is told over and over—it goes something like this:

A man by the name of Jesus once lived. One Friday He was crucified. After one of the soldiers had thrust a spear into His side to make sure He was dead, he probably turned away saying, "That one didn't take long." Simon Peter, one of Christ's followers, was heard to say, "I go a fishing." There was nothing else left to do. He had visions of Christ bringing in a Kingdom, but now He was dead. So

116

it was back to the little boat with its patched sails, back to mending the nets.

Came Sunday morning. Three women had come to anoint His body. They found the stone rolled away and His tomb empty. Two of the women left. "But Mary stood without at the sepulchre weeping" (John 20:11). She saw a man but did not recognize Him. Then He said, "Mary." The way He spoke her name! No one else had said it as He had. Just that one word, yet all of heaven was in it. She cried, "Master!" She knew. There was no doubt. It was He.

That afternoon some friends of His who lived in Emmaus recognized Him by the way He broke the bread. That same night, ten of the disciples were together when He appeared to them. They never doubted again. Eight days later, He invited Thomas to ". . . Reach hither thy finger, and behold my hands; and reach hither thy hand, and thrust it into my side: and be not faithless, but believing." Thomas answered, "My Lord and my God" (John 20:27, 28).

Others saw Him, some through their physical eyes and others, like St. Paul, through the reality of a spiritual experience. They went everywhere telling about His resurrection. It wasn't a story they invented. Would any man have invented such a story in order to be crucified upside down, as was Peter? Or to get his head chopped off, as did Paul? Or to be stoned to death, as was Stephen?

The Bible says, "Then were the disciples glad, when they saw the Lord" (John 20:20). The Greek word here for "see" does not mean to look through your physical eyes, as you look at a mountain, or at another person, or at the words on a printed page. The word "see" here means inner sight—perception—understanding.

"When the disciples saw!" They were never afraid again —not even of death. Peter was to be executed one morning at daybreak. The night before he did not pace the floor of his cell as some wild animal might have. Instead, he calmly lay down and went to sleep. When they observed the change in those who "saw," their enemies "marvelled; and they took knowledge of them, that they had been with Jesus" (Acts 4:13).

We, too, stand before an open grave. We see One standing by. He calls our name. We can never explain it; we only know it is true. We "see" the Lord and we hear Him saying, "because I live, ye shall live also." And we know it is true.

24.

ETERNAL LIFE

WHY DO SO many more people go to church on Easter Sunday than any other Sunday of the year? It is because Easter is the firmest hold that man has on life after death.

In Thornton Wilder's play, *Our Town*, one of the characters says: "I don't care what they say with their mouths —everybody knows that something is eternal. And it ain't houses, and it ain't names, and it ain't earth, and it ain't even stars . . . everybody knows in their bones that something is eternal, and that something has to do with human beings. All the greatest people ever lived have been telling us that for five thousand years and yet you'd be surprised how people are losing hold of it. There's something way down deep that's eternal about every human being."

That is true—"Everybody knows in their bones that something is eternal." We do not have to have a reason to believe it. It is intuition with us. We just know it. Yet, ". . . people are losing hold of it." Into our minds come doubts. Sometimes the thought of death puts panic into our hearts. We associate death with shadows and with darkness.

"Sunset and evening star, And one clear call for me!" we quote. Or we sing, "Abide with me: fast falls the eventide; The darkness deepens; Lord with me abide. . . ."

On Easter, we take hold again of the certainty of eternal life. We look to that day to take away the gloom and the fear, to give us comfort and assurance. I know there are some people who claim not to be interested in the life beyond. A friend of Maude Royden's said:

> Don't bother me now,
> Don't bother me never;
> I want to be dead
> Forever and ever.

After I had conducted the funeral service for a dear mother her little boy, less than ten years old, said to me, "Where's my Mamma now?" I might have said, "She's dead," but that would have been a sorry answer. Yet— without Easter I would have had no other answer. We come to church that day because there is an answer. The answer is the promise of Christ, "Because I live, ye shall live also." You find those words in the fourteenth chapter of St. John (14:19).

He begins that chapter with: "Let not your heart be troubled . . ." and he goes on to tell that beyond this life there is another abiding place. He says He will be there and that we will be with Him. But is that true? Can you believe it? Is there any proof? "Because I live," He said. On the fact of His resurrection rests man's assurance of life after death.

On Easter Sunday, in more than a thousand languages, we sing and say, "Christ, the Lord is risen today." But is it really true? How can we be sure?

REASONS WE ARE SURE

You believe there once lived a man by the name of Jesus. You are familiar with much that He said and did— how He offered a new way of life, performed miracles, and loved people. You know that He was put to death, but do you really believe that He lived again after death? You can say, "Yes, I believe that he rose from the dead" and yet not realize it.

One of the truly great preachers was Dr. A. W. Dale of England. His books have meant a great deal to me, but he had preached for years about Christ before the truth really

119

dawned upon him. Afterward he wrote: " 'Christ is alive,' I said to myself. 'Alive!' And then I paused: 'Alive!' Can that really be true? Living as I myself am? I got up and walked about repeating, 'Christ is living! Christ is living!' At first it seemed strange and hardly true, but at last it came upon me as a burst of sudden glory; yes, Christ is alive. It was to me a new discovery. I thought that all along I have believed it; but not until that moment did I feel sure about it."

How can we know, as Dr. Dale knew, that Christ is risen? There are two ways to know: (1) Through a study of the evidence; and (2) through an experience of His Presence. Our evidence is found in the last two chapters in each of the first three Gospels—Matthew, Mark, and Luke —and the last three chapters of John. He was pronounced dead. His body was embalmed. Remembering that He said He would rise, every possible precaution was taken to prevent a hoax or a fake. His body was placed in a grave hewn in solid rock and sealed with a large stone. The stone was so large that three women together could not move it.

A Roman guard of the finest soldiers the world had known was stationed to watch His grave. Then an earthquake came. An angel descended from heaven. Because of their fear, these soldiers did shake and become as dead men. Later it was suggested they fell asleep, but you cannot imagine an entire company of Roman soldiers falling asleep on duty. The noise of the stone moving would surely have wakened some.

His own followers did not expect Him to rise. Not even one of them expected it. If they had thought it was even a possibility, they would have been waiting around His tomb instead of shutting themselves up in a room, with the doors barred for fear. Even when they were told the news, they did not believe.

In fact, it took forty days for the Lord to convince them. During those forty days He appeared to them seven times that we know of. And then He ascended out of their sight. I think there is no greater proof of His resurrection than the change that took place in those men who knew Him best.

When He was buried they were depressed, frightened,

and filled with despair. Just seven weeks later, they were fearlessly shouting the news to every person who would listen. After Jesus ascended, they were men filled with joy and courage and with a vision of conquering the world in His name. The evidence of His resurrection was strong enough for those who were there.

THE SUPREME ASSURANCE

Jesus said, "Because I live, ye shall live also." We can know that He lived through studying the evidence of His death and resurrection. But that is not sufficient. St. Paul never saw Christ in the flesh. He heard the stories of His resurrection. In the fifteenth chapter of First Corinthians, which incidentally is the greatest statement on life after death that has ever been made, he records the fact that:

After His resurrection, Christ ". . . was seen of Cephas, then of the twelve: After that, he was seen of above five hundred brethren at once; of whom the greater part remain unto this present, but some are fallen asleep. After that, he was seen of James; then of all the apostles" (15:5-7).

But for a long time Paul did not believe that preponderance of testimony. In fact, the stories of Jesus angered and upset him. To him the followers of Christ were fanatics, and Paul did all he could to put an end to their talk and activity. Then one day Paul watched as one of the Christians named Stephen was stoned. There was something in the way Stephen died that disturbed Paul. Stephen had something that Paul knew he didn't have.

And we, too, have seen this "something" in the lives of other people. We have observed in certain ones who profess to be Christians a radiance, a goodness, a quality of character and life that is different. We know of those who have sacrificed in the support of His work, and maybe we have wondered why they would do it. Yet even this does not completely convince us.

Finally St. Paul said, "And last of all he was seen of me also, as one born out of due time" (15:8). As Paul made his way along the Damascus road, his conscience bothered him (Acts 9:1-6). He felt that he was not living the life he should. He wasn't easy in his mind about it. Suddenly light from heaven began to shine around him. Then a voice began to speak asking why he kept on rebelling and not doing what he knew he should do? Then Paul said, "Lord, what wilt thou have me to do?" (Acts 9:6).

He surrendered his rebellious will. He began to live and do as he felt Christ wanted him to. From then on he lived for Christ. At the end of his life he was in jail and soon to be executed. But he was not worried. Instead, he wrote to his young friend Timothy and told him, "Fight the good fight of faith, lay hold on eternal life . . ." (I Timothy 6:12).

And today, as we "fight the good fight of faith," we come into a realization that Christ does live. We joyously sing: "He lives, He lives, salvation to impart. . . . You ask me how I know He lives? . . . He lives within my heart." And because we know He lives, we can say even as the great Apostle said, "O death, where is thy sting? O grave, where is thy victory? . . . thanks be to God, which giveth us the victory through our Lord Jesus Christ" (I Corinthians 15:55, 57).

25.

WHAT THE BIBLE SAYS ABOUT HEAVEN

WHAT DOES the Bible say about heaven? Down through the centuries, man has wondered about heaven and wanted to know more about it. The Psalmist looked into the skies and was so impressed by them that he declared, "The heavens declare the glory of God . . ." (19:1).

In every possible way, mankind has sought answers to his questions about the heavens. We have built giant telescopes to pierce the outer spaces and space ships that lift one miles and miles above the earth. We have learned a lot about the lands of the sky, yet the heavens are still mysterious. We say with the poet, "Twinkle, twinkle little star, how I wonder what you are."

We know that no telescope can see the heaven we are most interested in, neither will any space ship ever be able to ascend to its pearly gates. The only reliable information we have about heaven is what the Bible says. I spent an entire evening recently reading in the Bible about heaven. When I got through, a lot of my questions were *not* fully answered.

We wish the Bible told us such things as: Will babies who die always be babies in heaven? Will old people who die always remain old? Will we see and recognize each other there? Will we miss people who are not there? What sort of activity goes on in heaven? What happens during the interval between leaving this world and arriving in the next? Even if we find the answers to these questions, we want to know more.

How big a place is heaven? Today approximately two billion people die every thirty years. When we think of all who have died since Adam and all who will die in the future centuries, could even the universe be big enough to hold them all? Do people in heaven know what people on earth are doing? Can they communicate with us? Could one come back to earth, if he wished to? I find no specific answer to any of those questions in the Bible, yet we find the answer to all our questions as we read the holy Book.

MAN IS NOT AT HOME ON EARTH

To begin with, we see in the Bible how God has put into man a restlessness in this world. The Psalmist said, "I am a stranger in the earth . . ." (119:19) and St. Paul declares, "We are . . . willing rather to be absent from the body, and to be present with the Lord" (II Corinthians 5:8). Man is essentially a spiritual being and can never be completely at rest in this world. An old song says,

I am a stranger here, within a foreign land;
My home is far away, upon a golden strand. . . .
I'm here on business for my king.

Something in man is always seeking a fuller life. Earth never completely satisfies him. Other creatures seem to fit into the world of nature, but man is constantly looking for something else. I spend a lot of nights in hotels, but it isn't like being at home. And the Bible tells us that heaven is our home, the end of the journey.

HEAVEN IS A PLACE PREPARED

What is heaven like? Jesus said, "In my Father's house are many mansions [rooms]" (John 14:2). How many is many? Some people have mighty narrow thoughts about it. They think heaven is a tiny little place reserved especially for them and a few people who think as they do.

The Bible tells us there are twelve gates opening in every direction (Revelation 21:12, 13) and streaming in through those gates is a multitude so great that no man can number them. They come from all nations and they are all kinds of people (Revelation 7:9). What a rebuke to our narrow prejudices and our selfish exclusiveness!

Also Jesus said, "I go to prepare a place for you" (John 14:2). Each person has a distinctive place both in the Father's heart and in the Father's house. You will still be you over there. When parents have a son who lives in another city and he is expected home for a visit, Mamma puts clean sheets on his bed, prepares the dinner she knows he will like, and does everything possible to make him happy at home. Likewise Christ says, "I go to prepare a place for you." It will be a place we will like.

Why did He not tell us more about that place? I think the reason is, if He had, it would at this time really not appeal to us. The Bible tells us that in heaven ". . . we shall all be changed" (I Corinthians 15:51). That is not surprising. We are constantly changing. When I was a little boy, the railroad ran in front of our house. I watched the big engines go by and wished I could ride with the engineer.

124

That would have made me so happy. Once I was taking a train trip. I knew the engineer and asked if I might ride with him for a time. He let me, but I was disappointed. The experience that would have thrilled me so as a little boy now was dull for me.

Man has an amazing capacity for growth. He only begins to touch his possibilities here on this earth. In heaven are lifted the limitations of the flesh and we reach our highest and best selves. We think in terms of little pleasures here. We satisfy ourselves with earthly joys. But when we become fully developed we will have capacities to enjoy so much that we cannot even conceive of now. So we are told, "... Eye hath not seen, nor ear heard, neither have entered into the heart of man, the things which God hath prepared for them that love him" (I Corinthians 2:9). Jesus did not tell us more simply because we would not now understand or appreciate it. Sufficient is the fact that He is preparing for us—each one of us.

Since my wife and I have been married, we have lived in ten different houses. I don't remember how many chairs there were in any living room we ever had or the color of a single rug in any house we have lived in. I have never paid much attention to the furniture we had, but many nights I have driven across the state to get back to one of those houses. Why was I so anxious to get to that house? Because my wife was there and our children were there, and my loved ones being there is what made it home. And I want to know if we will be together in heaven.

WE WILL KNOW EACH OTHER THERE

Will we know each other in heaven? That is the main question about eternity that we want answered. After the death of his wife, Robert Browning wrote his lovely poem, "Prospice," in which he said:

> O thou soul of my soul! I shall clasp thee again,
> And with God be the rest.

Just to clasp her again would have been heaven for him.

Charles Kingsley selected the words for his tombstone: *Amavimus, Amamus, Amabimus*—"We have loved, we do love, we shall love." The love of his life here, he did not expect to lose over there.

But this brings up complications. Some men asked Jesus, what if a woman were married several times, whose wife would she be in the resurrection? That question worries people today who have had more than one wife or husband. And the matter of family reunions in heaven is hard to understand. Will my wife be with her father and mother, and will I be with mine? Then what about our children and our family?

Jesus said that in heaven we "neither marry, nor are given in marriage . . ." (Matthew 22:30). The problem exists because we think in terms of physical relationships and heaven is on a higher plane. Love in heaven is not less real, but more real. Surely we will know each other there. The Bible doesn't directly discuss the matter of recognition in heaven; it just assumes it.

As Jesus talked with His disciples about the Father's house, He said, ". . . if it were not so, I would have told you" (John 14:2). Surely He who did so much to strengthen human love on earth would have told us if we are to lose that which is most precious to us.

As our Lord hung on the cross, He spoke to one dying by His side. He didn't say, "Well, I hope to see you again." Neither did He say, "We might see each other again." He said, ". . . Today shalt thou be with me . . ." (Luke 23:43). We are the same people over there. Moses and Elijah had been dead for centuries when they came back to visit with Christ on the Mount of Transfiguration. But they were still the same. We will love each other again and all the problems we can think of have already been solved.

I have no worries about heaven when I read John's vision in Revelation 4:2, 3. He says, ". . . behold, a throne was set in heaven, and one sat on the throne. . . . and there was a rainbow round about the throne. . . ." A throne signifies authority, law and order. Heaven is not a place of chaos. On the throne is the Father and that means His will is being done. Everything there is perfectly as it should be.

The rainbow means the storms are past; it is the symbol

of hope beyond the tragedies. Here on earth we have troubles and heartaches, but there everything is all right. On earth man has done his worst; over there God has done His best—and nothing could be better than God's best. God is on the throne with a rainbow round about—nothing needs to be said beyond that.

From the jungles of Ecuador to a tiny watchshop in Holland to behind the Iron Curtain—thrill to the very real human drama of ordinary people who suddenly find themselves empowered by God's love to do *extraordinary* things . . .

____**THROUGH GATES OF SPLENDOR.** Five young Americans travel to Ecuador to build bridges: from paganism to Christian belief. *Elliott.* $1.25 paper

____**THE HIDING PLACE.** A Dutch spinster's world is turned upside down when she begins to hide Jews during World War II. *ten Boom.* $1.50 paper, $1.75 paper Movie Edition

____**GOD'S SMUGGLER.** In the face of tremendous odds, one man takes on the daring mission of smuggling Bibles across the Iron Curtain. *Andrew.* $1.25 paper

____**THE PERSECUTOR.** How a Soviet secret police member comes to embrace the faith of those he formerly persecuted. *Kourdakov.* $1.50 paper

ORDER FROM YOUR BOOKSTORE

If your bookstore does not stock these books, order from
SPIRE BOOKS
Box 150, Old Tappan, New Jersey 07675
Please send me the books I've checked above. Enclosed is my payment plus 25¢ mailing charge on first book ordered, 10¢ each additional book.

NAME_____

STREET_____

CITY_____ STATE_____ ZIP_____

____Amount enclosed. ____Cash. ____Check. ____Money order. (No c.o.d.'s)